PARANORMAL APOCALYPSE

IS THIS HOW IT ENDS?

MAXIM W. FUREK

HANGAR 1 PUBLISHING

Paranormal Apocalypse: Is this How it Ends? by Maxim W. Furek
FIRST EDITION. First printing, 2025
Copyright © 2024 by Maxim W. Furek
Contact information at www.maximfurek.com

Cover and page designs by Hangar 1 Publishing. Back inside photo by Patricia A. Furek.
Back cover drawing of Death, one of the Four Horsemen of the Apocalypse, by
permission of Travis McHenry.

Hangar 1 Publishing.
11610 Jay St NW
Minneapolis, MN, 55448
Printed in the United States of America.

This book is dedicated to my good friend and mentor, Dr. Ted Billy (1947-2022), an exceptional American gothic scholar and authority on Edgar Allan Poe, H.P. Lovecraft, and Joseph Conrad. Ted was a true gentleman, a kind soul, and an inspiration to all who knew him. RIP.

QR EXPERIENCE INSTRUCTIONS

To operate the QR codes within the pages, simply point any smartphone at the QR code square like you are going to take a photo. Your phone should immediately prompt you to the link needed to access the bonus multi-media content. Click that link. Headphones or earbuds are suggested for an optimal audio experience.

As with children and animals, we share fear and curiosity in equal measure. The moth to the flame. The rat to the cheese. The spider watching the fly. Fear captivates and mesmerizes and can only be contained through Apocalyptic Awe.

— MAXIM W. FUREK

CONTENTS

IN THE YEAR 2525 (EXORDIUM & TERMINUS)

In the year 2525, if man is still alive
If woman can survive, they may find

In the year 3535
Ain't gonna need to tell the truth, tell no lie
Everything you think, do and say
Is in the pill you took today

In the year 4545
You ain't gonna need your teeth, won't need your eyes
You won't find a thing to chew
Nobody's gonna look at you

In the year 5555
Your arms hangin' limp at your sides
Your legs got nothin' to do
Some machine's doin' that for you

In the year 6565
You won't need no husband, won't need no wife

You'll pick your son, pick your daughter too
From the bottom of a long glass tube

In the year 7510
If God's a coming, He oughta make it by then
Maybe He'll look around Himself and say
Guess it's time for the judgment day

In the year 8510
God is gonna shake His mighty head
He'll either say I'm pleased where man has been
Or tear it down, and start again

In the year 9595
I'm kinda wonderin' if man is gonna be alive
He's taken everything this old earth can give
And he ain't put back nothing

Now it's been ten thousand years
Man has cried a billion tears
For what, he never knew, now man's reign is through
But through eternal night, the twinkling of starlight
So very far away, maybe it's only yesterday

In the year 2525, if man is still alive
If woman can survive, they may find

ZAGER & EVANS

Produced by Zager & Evans

STEREO

74-0174

Victor

Zelad Music
BMI
XPKS-5615

3:15

IN THE YEAR 2525
(Exordium & Terminus)
(Evans)
TMK(s) ® REGISTERED • MARCA(s) REGISTRADA(s)
RADIO CORPORATION OF AMERICA—MADE IN U.S.A

In the Year 2525: RCA Victor Records, Public domain, via Wikimedia Commons.

Question: You begin your book with a classic rock song from 1969? With this chapter, are you wearing the hat of a rock journalist or paranormal researcher?

2

EXORDIUM & TERMINUS

As a former rock journalist, the sound of music has always been a part of me, a constant companion that has reverberated in my head and flowed through my veins. Its echoes are always there, as strong today as they were yesterday, like a childhood friend. This book is a testament to the enduring nature of music in my life. As a Baby Boomer, I was captivated by the song *In the Year 2525*, not only for its disturbing content and seductive musicality, but also for its unexpectedness. The song didn't fit in with the era's zeitgeist, one that day-tripped on tie-dyed acid dreams and psychedelia. The song was a jarring anomaly that prophesied societal collapse and doom, a fitting preface to this book.

Recorded in a cow pasture studio in Odessa, Texas and written by Rick Evans in just 10 minutes, *In the Year 2525 (Exordium & Terminus)* was recorded by the American duo of Zager and Evans. It only took three weeks for it to reach the top spot on U.S. charts, hanging there for six weeks, from July 12 to August 16, 1969.

The record was awarded a gold disc by the Recording Industry Association of America (RIAA) in July 1969 and had sold over 4 million copies by 1970. It has been covered over 60 times and in seven languages. 2525 enshrined Zager and Evans as masters of the fabled one-hit wonder. More importantly, the song represented one of the best descriptions of the end of the world, as noted by *Billboard*:

> *Presenting a dystopian view of the future, the song explores the consequences of human's overreliance on technology. It suggests that if we continue this trend, we might be facing our own destruction in a few years' time. The song paints a picture of a sad world where nature is gone, individuality is lost, and we are disconnected from each other. The singer plays with the idea that by the year 7510, God might bring down judgment day.*

Still, the song's popularity made little sense. 2525 was a stranger in a strange land, far removed from the heartbeat of the 1960s. First, the song happened in 1969, when American astronauts walked on the moon in awe and 400,000 hippies gathered in Bethel, New York for the Woodstock Aquarian and Art Festival. And two, this was the era of "Make Love, Not War." The tidal waves of flower power and psychedelia were rushing over us in seas of peace, protest, and LSD.

Aside from all that, the real question is, how did a miserable song about humankind's finality boogie-woogie onto the *Billboard* charts while we were tripping out to Quicksilver Messenger Service, Jefferson Airplane, and the Grateful Dead? How did that happen on our watch? Rock music has always been about rebellion and teenage angst, but this song smacked of damnation, doom, and incongruity. Author Tom Reynolds' *I Hate Myself and Want to Die: The 52 Most Depressing Songs You've Ever Heard* (2005) took note of the song's joylessness:

> *In the Year 2525 is a song about the journey of mankind over a 10,000-year span. It predicts that man's thoughts, relationships, and body will be negatively impacted by technological advances and ends with man's extinction.*

Rick Evans died in February 2018, after retiring from public life. But Denny Zager remained engaged in the music industry, building high-end custom guitars in Lincoln, Nebraska, comparable to the Gibsons, Martins, and Taylors that he grew up with.

When 2525 hit number one in the U.S. and U.K. and number two in Australia, Zager and Evans became the *only* act in history to score a number one on both sides of the Atlantic—yet they would never chart in the U.K. or U.S. again. While 2525 is an enduring piece of music history, similarly, it is a classic example of Apocalyptic Awe—the embracing of the end times in popular films, books, and music and the most important contributor to the genre's collective consciousness. There were other—maybe not as controversial or provocative—apocalyptic songs that made us swoon and dance as we contemplated the worst of times. Skeeter Davis' double-tracked signature song, *It's the End of the World* (1962), was "one of the greatest songs ever about the aftermath of a devastating loss." On Davis' song, Jim Beviglia, writing for *American Songwriter*, noted that:

> The End of the World *deals with the notion of how losing someone from your life can cause a kind of disconnect when the rest of your surroundings insist on continuing without interruption. The opening lines lay out the premise, as Davis wonders, why does the sun go on shining? Why does the sea rush to shore?*

The video clip for *Die with A Smile* (2025), the commercially successful hit by Lady GaGa and Bruno Mars, conjured up a musical apocalypse with the phrase "nobody's promised tomorrow," as observed by Sam Armstrong:

> *The clip crosses the billion mark less than nine months after its release last August. Since then it has topped the Billboard Hot 100 for five weeks, been included on Gaga's new album* Mayhem, *and won the Grammy for Best Pop Duo/Group Performance.*

Some believe the Day of Reckoning is upon us, shrouded in trepidation and hope, misery and balance. Armageddon will be fought in the Garden of Eden, where the rebellion against God began. After the final battle between the sons of God and the demons of Satan, the earthly nectar will no longer be savored, as prophesied by the Four Horsemen of the Apocalypse. This powerful symbol of the end times is evident in countless medieval woodcuts, paintings, and manuscripts. One of the Bible's Book of Revelation's most iconic depictions is Albrecht Dürer's woodcut series, *The Apocalypse* (1498), which captured the chaos and destruction of the Four Horsemen. Michelangelo's fresco *The Last Judgment in the Sistine Chapel* (1536–1541) illustrated the moment Christ allows the blessed to rise toward heaven as the damned are dragged down into hell. And Salvador Dalí's *The Hallucinogenic Toreador* included subtle references to Revelation.

Apocalyptical books, too, provide vocabulary, imagery, and possible answers. Some have attained "classic" status, such as H.G. Wells' *War of the Worlds* (1898), Nevil Shute's *On the Beach* (1957), Philip K. Dick's *Do Androids Dream of Electric Sheep?* (1968), Stephen King's *The Stand* (1978), Max Brooks' *World War Z; An Oral History of the Zombie War* (2006), Suzanne Collins' *The Hunger Games* (2008), and Justin Cronin's *The Passage* (2010). Cormack McCarthy's *The Road* (2006) stood apart from the rest in searching for truth beyond human survival. It wasn't only about staying alive; it was about a father, a son, and a single bullet.

Rather than being celebrated as important cultural treasure, Apocalyptic Awe is at times castigated and censored. George Orwell's dystopian novel *Nineteen Eighty-Four* (1949), was banned in the U.S. for being pro-Communism and in Russia for being anti-Communism.

Although sadly ignored as an essential part of the genre, John Steinbeck's *The Grapes of Wrath* (1939) is perhaps the most realistic portrayal of the American Dust Bowl apocalypse that forced hundreds of thousands of penniless migrants to California's promised land. Steinbeck's title was derived from several sources including the Book of Revelation with images of grapes being crushed under God's wrath.

Even though the book was later awarded the Pulitzer Prize, it was removed from library shelves and classrooms and burned in places, including Kern County, California—the end point of the Joad family's migration. Calling Steinbeck a "Red" and a Communist, numerous groups attempted to ban his book because of objectionable issues such as: (1) Its portrayal of poverty and social injustice. (2) Business owners and landowners opposed the novel's endorsement of labor unionization, fearing its impact on their workers. (3) Parents and teachers criticized the book for explicit language, sexual content, and violence. (4) The Associated Farmers of California declared the novel a "pack of lies" and "Jewish propaganda." (5) The book was considered offensive because of its perceived communist sympathies and promotion of socialism and unionization. (6) Because of its portrayal of a stillborn child and the offering of breast milk to a dying stranger, the book's conclusion is considered indecent.

Eve of Destruction

Released on Truth Records in 1968, 2525 was picked up by RCA Records. The song followed in the wake of Barry McGuire's *Eve of Destruction* (1965), which touched on Cold War paranoia, racism, and environmental degradation. Songwriter P.F. Sloan's lyrics were banned by some American radio stations, claiming it was an "aid to the enemy in Vietnam."

Following the September 11, 2001 Al-Qaida attacks on New York's Twin Towers, 2525 was cited in a memo distributed by Clear Channel Communications to over 1,170 radio stations. The memo contained 165 songs considered "lyrically questionable." An advisory list of songs "which stations might wish to avoid playing in the short term," were compiled by Clear Channel program directors:

After and during what was happening in New York and Washington and outside of Pittsburgh, some of our program directors began e-mailing each other about songs and questionable song titles. Given the environment, a Clear Channel program director took it upon himself to identify a number of songs that certain markets or individuals may find insensitive today. This was not a mandate, nor was the list generated out of the corporate radio offices. It was a grassroots effort that was apparently circulated among program directors.

Controversy and admonition are the hallmarks of 2525, and Apocalyptic Awe has never been so well served. Similar warnings of a technological Armageddon were later made by Unabomber Ted Kaczynski in his 35,000-page manifesto:

Technological progress will eventually result in 'extensive genetic engineering of human beings, so that man in the future will no longer be a creation of nature, or of chance or of God.' Then, technology will have 'complete control over everything on Earth.'

Kaczynski's 1995 manifesto was widely read, especially within the Cyber Deep State, where it inspired violence by individuals like Luigi Mangione. Still, in the aftermath of violence lies the potential for rebirth, and if we make it out alive, it will be because of hope, resilience, and the human spirit.

Apocalyptic Awe provides all of that, offering an important composite of eight metaphysical and psychological variables: (1) Instruction and positive distraction. (2) A healthy form of fantasy and escapism. (3) An opportunity to explore uncertainty about impending pandemics and terrorism. (4) Promotion of dialogue, alternative perspectives, and critical thinking. (5) A platform to protest societal issues such as fossil fuels and global warming. (6) A cautionary tale warning of uncontrolled technology. (7) A means to promote political action and involvement in the democratic process. (8) A strategy that paradoxically reconnects us to our sense of self by focusing on external stimuli.

2525 is mired in the middle of all of that and remains exceptional in countless ways. At the very least, the song forms the *Exordium & Terminus* of this book—a symbolic homage to two singers from Nebraska and to a quintessential ode to the apocalypse. This song is a reminder of the impermanence of life and the need to enjoy the music of the moment.

This is the book I needed to write. It's the umbrella under which my other books stand and the sphere containing the things that have influenced and shaped my personal view of the world. *Paranormal Apocalypse* is the electricity that will hopefully allow each reader to find his or her own personal light in these times of darkness and provide enough information for the reader to begin a search of their own.

3

H.P. LOVECRAFT—SOOTHSAYER

The dark visionary, Howard Phillips Lovecraft (1890–1937), belonged to an earlier time when ladies and gentlemen strolled through Victorian gardens in airs of proper etiquette and respectability, when families of wealth were bowed down to and afforded their rightful place in society. But Lovecraft walked the streets like a man from Mars, an individual born too late, and filled with fear and racist hatred. He was awkward and reclusive, feeling like an orphan, and dying destitute and emotionally ruined.

And yet, Lovecraft endures as one of the most influential writers. His mythos of shadow worlds, interstellar deities, and "cosmic indifferentism" have inspired generations of storytellers, including Stephen King, Clive Barker, Neil Gaiman, and Anne Rice. And although acknowledged as the "Godfather of modern horror," he signifies much more. Lovecraft was a soothsayer, peering into the future and warning us with his cryptic prose.

Lovecraft scholar Miranda Gurzo observed that "Lovecraftian literature is full of apocalyptic suggestions from the very beginning," such as Cthulhu, the tentacle-faced elder god who lies slumbering in his oceanic tomb, waiting for the day when "the stars are right" to rise again and wreak havoc on humanity. Lovecraft's prophecies were acknowledged by Joyce Carol Oates, an avid student of the horror master:

> Lovecraft fuses the supernatural and mundane into a terrifying, complex, and exquisitely realized vision, foretelling a psychically troubled century to come.

As Edgar Allen Poe draped us in a Gothic sheath, Lovecraft cast a wider net, foretelling the indescribable insanity of never being able to comprehend that which is not meant for the human mind. He was precocious—reciting poetry at age two, reading at three, and writing at six or seven. His earliest enthusiasm was for *The Arabian Nights*, Greek mythology, and weird fiction. His grandfather, Whipple Van Buren Phillips, fostered his interest, entertaining Lovecraft with weird Gothic ghost stories.

Like influential editor Ray A. Palmer, Lovecraft sought refuge in the escapism of literature, especially the fantasies of Lord Dunsany and Alfred Lord Tennyson. Inspired by Poe, about 80 years his senior, Lovecraft began dabbling in amateur journalism. Many of his stories were featured in pulp magazines like *Weird Tales* and influenced by post-World War I horrors of mustard gas and trench warfare. Lovecraft wrote about "cosmic horror," a mix of forgotten elder beings and slimy alien gods. Cthulhu, the leader of the Great Old Ones, was described as:

> A monster of vaguely anthropoid outline, but with an octopus-like head whose face was a mass of feelers, a scaly, rubbery-looking body, prodigious claws on hind and fore feet, and long, narrow wings behind. It is said to be so terrible to behold that it destroys the sanity of those who see it.

As Poe wrapped us in layers of fear, Lovecraft gave us equal parts of hopelessness and uncertainty. A favorite Lovecraft touch was of the obsessive researcher who, by unleashing an interdimensional evil, threatens to wipe out the planet as he is rendered insane. Lovecraft's concept of the Great Old Ones was indescribable, said Lovecraft scholar John DeLaughter:

> *They sprang forth as primal shadows cast from the dawn of time. They embodied the fears of our ancestors. No one species, no tribal god, no one alien race, no ancient taboo nor obscure pantheon explained them. They expressed the tangible dark, the teeming life in the shadows, life without light. Though everyone knows them, no one living has seen them. They are vague shadows that shift and scurry in the dark abyss, like amoebas in pond water.*

The Colour Out of Space

Most of his stories occurred in New England, where he invented the fictional town of Arkham, Massachusetts, and prestigious Miskatonic University. His most famous literary invention was the *Necronomicon*, a forbidden book of dark magic incorporated into additional stories by other writers.

During his lifetime, he wrote an estimated 100,000 letters to friends and fellow writers such as Robert Bloch, Henry Kuttner, and Robert E. Howard, and his Mythos has been embellished and reinterpreted by countless writers such as Bloch, Clark Ashton Smith, and August Derleth. *The Colour Out of Space*, published in the September 1927 edition of Hugo Gernsback's *Amazing Stories*, describes an area known by the locals as "the blasted heath," outside the fictional town of Arkham, where a meteorite has crashed, poisoning or killing every living thing. *The Colour Out of Space* provided a template adapted to film several times, in incarnations such as *Die, Monster, Die!* (1965), *The Curse* (1987), *Colour from the Dark* (2008), *The Colour Out of Space (Die Farbe)* (2010), and *Color Out of Space* (2019). Lovecraft's story inspired Stephen King's 1987 novel *The Tommyknockers*—in which the residents of Haven, Maine, fall under the influence of a long-buried alien spacecraft in the woods.

Personal Demons

Born into an affluence that was abruptly ripped away, Lovecraft lived in near poverty, often skipping meals to afford writing materials and postage. He claimed to be so poor that he survived for days on one loaf of bread, one can of cold beans, and a hunk of cheese. As he walked the streets of his beloved Providence, he languished in the shadows of the better-known Poe and suffered an endless battle with his personal demons. Avoiding people, he routinely slept late into the day, only leaving the house after sunset. His complexion turned pale and gaunt. His mother, Sarah Susan Phillips Lovecraft, called her son "grotesque" and "hideous" and warned him to hide inside so people couldn't see him. In 1908, he suffered a nervous breakdown just before his graduation from Hope High School. Depressed, he left school without a diploma, and his rejection from Brown University caused him considerable shame. Though one of the most formidable self-taught academics of his era, he spent ages 18 to 23 as a virtual hermit, immersed in astronomy and poetry:

> I am essentially a recluse who will have very little to do with people wherever he may be. I think that most people only make me nervous—that only by accident, and in extremely small quantities, would I ever be likely to come across people who wouldn't.

Apocalyptic parables have prophesized the expectant hand of death. Throughout the ages, the masses have feared these adult fairy tales threatening the consequences of our wickedness:

> Because we have sinned, we will be punished. Because of our sins, we deserve to be punished. And because we are sinners, the future will be filled with pain and suffering.

Those parables, it would seem, had been written for the Lovecraft family who suffered from mental illness and were cursed with genetics that perverted reality. His father was institutionalized at Providence's Butler Hospital for the Insane and died there five years later, as documented by *The Guardian*'s Sian Cain:

Winfield Scott Lovecraft was committed to Butler Hospital after being diagnosed with psychosis when H.P. Lovecraft was only three years old. He died in 1898, when H.P. was eight. To this day, rumours persist that Winfield had syphilis, but neither H.P. nor his mother ever displayed symptoms.

Death Diary

H.P. Lovecraft: The "Godfather of modern horror" is one of the most influential of writers, inspiring generations of storytellers, as both soothsayer and dark visionary.

The darkness continued. Lovecraft was 28 when his mother was admitted to the same hospital treating her husband. They remained in close correspondence for two years, until she died of complications after surgery. After marrying businesswoman Sonia Greene in 1924, he lived briefly in Brooklyn, where he wrote *The Horror at Red Hook*, one of his most blatantly racist stories. The racism that Lovecraft harbored was rampant in many parts of the country and would continue long after his death in 1937. During the Reconstruction era (1865–1876), nearly 2,000 Black men, women, and children were lynched. In 1921, the Tulsa Race Massacre—one of the worst racial attacks in U.S. history—left as many as 300 Black people dead and destroyed the once-thriving district of North Tulsa, later purposefully erased from history books. Decades later, in 1998, James Byrd Jr., a 49-year-old Black man, was chained to a pickup truck and dragged to his death by three white men. Racism aside, after his marriage ended, Lovecraft returned to his Providence sanctuary, completing the novellas *The Shadow Over Innsmouth* and *At the Mountains of Madness*.

At 46, he began to create a "Death Diary," recording his daily sufferings as he died from stomach cancer. "Pain—drowse—intense pain—rest—great pain," he wrote in one entry, an intimate moment of torment echoed in his short story *The Haunter of the Dark*, written that same year, in which one of the protagonists continues to write in his journal even as the dreadful monster closes in:

> *I see it—coming here—hell-wind—titan blur—black wings—Yog-Sothoth save me—the three-lobed burning eye...*

Lovecraft expressed a contempt for "savage and uneducated immigrants" lacking honored social protocols. In countless personal letters, he expressed displeasure with anything outside his beloved Providence, where he retreated from his estranged wife, Sonia, and those immigrant hordes. There is little doubt that he was a racist, xenophobe, and white supremacist. His views, unfortunate as they were, reflected the thinking of the time. He predicted that the Chinese empire of Tsan Chan would flourish in 5000 AD and that the "evil and yellow" faces of the Chinese would replace Western people in an apocalyptic nightmare.

Gazing into an antiquated crystal ball, Lovecraft foresaw the demise of a "cold and ruthless" Western civilization, rotting away from nihilism, consumerism, and a rejection of what was considered Dark Age superstition. Seven decades after his death, the impact of his extreme views has not lessened. Lovecraft must be turning in his grave at the "capitalistic success story" merchandizing his weird mythos. As Damon Root discerned in his *Reason* essay, *The Uncanny Afterlife of H.P. Lovecraft*:

Retailers now offer Cthulhu-themed shirts, hats, socks, costumes, toys, coffee mugs, Pez dispensers, board games, video games, role-playing games, novels, short stories, comic books, coloring books, and much else besides. The heavy metal band Metallica has written two songs in Cthulhu's honor. The Oscar-winning director Guillermo del Toro has found all sorts of clever ways to reference Cthulhu in his films.

Lovecraft has been regarded as the most influential figure in modern horror fiction. Writer Jeffrey Somers articulated what the "Father of Modern Horror" brought to the table—Lovecraft changed the rules, usurping a genre that was still bound to Victorian and Gothic restrictions and introduced into it a truly frightening concept:

That the universe wasn't filled with rule-obeying evil you could comprehend and thus defeat; rather, it was filled with beings and forces so beyond us they aren't even aware of our existence as they terrify, destroy, and annihilate us.

The Cthulhu Mythos

Lovecraft stands alone as history's foremost innovator of science fiction horror. Years after his death from small-intestine cancer, he was acknowledged as a major contributor, having created unique and unorthodox characters from his own vision. He listened to the music of Erich Zann and to the rats in the wall while gazing at forbidden cosmos. But everything about Lovecraft's path was slightly out of step. The independent Arkham House didn't publish his first major book, *The Outsider and Others* (1939), until two years after his death, and his second book, *Beyond the Wall of Sleep* (1943), four years after that. Founded by Lovecraft devotees August Derleth and Donald Wandrei, Arkham House was created for the sole purpose of keeping their hero's work in print. Another obscure footnote is that Lovecraft ghostwrote the 1924 short story *Imprisoned with the Pharaohs* for escape artist Harry Houdini. His notoriety, like a fistful of missing pages from one of his weird tales, came later, as observed by Pat Bauer, writing in Britannica:

> *Though Lovecraft did not live long enough to see the success of his work, in the decades following his death, other authors began writing stories about the Cthulhu Mythos. They included Robert Bloch, Stephen King, Neil Gaiman, and Alan Moore. By the turn of the 21st century, the Cthulhu Mythos had become a cultural phenomenon.*

Lovecraft dreamed of dark gods who rebelled against science, and the Cthulhu Mythos was his most dynamic creation. It was invented by his disciple August Derleth, and inspired by Alfred Lord Tennyson (1809–1892), who published the 15-line sonnet *The Kraken* (1830), with its vivid imagery of a sea monster sleeping for an eternity at the bottom of the ocean and destined to emerge from its slumber in an apocalyptic age:

> *Below the thunders of the upper deep,*
> *Far, far beneath in the abysmal sea,*
> *His ancient, dreamless, uninvaded sleep*
> *The Kraken sleepeth:*
> *Faintest sunlights flee about his shadowy sides;*
> *Above him swell Huge sponges of millennial growth and height;*
> *And far away into the sickly light...*

The Cthulhu Mythos has become one of horror literature's most mined themes, as witnessed in the works of hundreds of writers, specifically *The Children of Lovecraft*, as well as in music, horror movies, board and card games, and tabletop role-playing games. There is even a popular "Cthulhu for President" bumper sticker asking, "Why vote for the lesser evil?"

In her comprehensive 2018, *A monstrous primer on the works of H.P.*

Lovecraft: Your guide to the fantasy author's nightmarish must-reads, Emma Stefansky observed:

> *Lovecraft pioneered the "speculative fiction" genre and started the Cosmicism movement, which is marked by the belief that there are interstellar beings far outside the realm of human perception and that humans are an insignificant part of a very large, very terrifying universe. His narrators are unreliable, often addicted to substances, their minds altered and broken by the horrors they've witnessed.*

Lovecraft introduced the concept of "alien" into our vocabulary, not bulb-headed grays from another planet, but creatures with slimy tentacles who had dwelled on Earth for millions of years. He assaulted us with apocalyptic visions that had yet to be considered. Blending pseudoscience with terror, Lovecraft's premise replicated like a contagion, as revealed in the opening sentences of his signature story, *The Call of Cthulhu:*

> *The most merciful thing in the world, I think, is the inability of the human mind to correlate all its contents. We live on a placid island of ignorance in the midst of black seas of infinity, and it was not meant that we should voyage far.*

Lovecraft's Great Old Ones possessed shapes that the human mind was incapable of processing. By simply viewing them, the viewer is rendered incurably insane, such as in his first short story, *Dagon* (1917). In his narrative, ancient remnants prove that alien civilizations have visited us. Lovecraft's works "traditionally feature humans catching glimpses of a bigger universe our minds were never built to comprehend," such as in *At the Mountains of Madness* and *The Colour Out of Space.* In *Dagon*, the protagonist is unable to accept the horrors witnessed on an unknown Pacific island. In this story, the unfortunate narrator, after confronting a specimen of an unknown race of aquatic monsters, approaches madness, fearing:

The day when they come out of the waves and clasp in immense claws the remains of insignificant humanity worn out by wars... the day the lands will sink and the dark bottom of the oceans will rise to the surface, in universal pandemonium.

Lovecraft's Great Old Ones reflected personal trauma and anticipation of the end times, fashioned from a backdrop of lost family wealth, mental instability, and hatred of foreigners. As Lovecraft envisioned, these deities once ruled the Earth but have since fallen into a death-like coma. They were indifferent to weak and irrelevant humans and worshipped by deranged human cults. In his Mythos, the Great Old Ones and Other Gods are ruled by Azathoth (the Blind Idiot God who holds court at the center of infinity) and Nyarlathotep (the Crawling Chaos), and lesser gods including Shub-Niggurath (the Black Goat of the Woods with a Thousand Young) and Yog-Sothoth (the All-in-One and One-in-All).

Question: Why do you cite HP Lovecraft as the only individual to adequately explain the mechanism of fear?

His imagination inspired a new definition of horror. The term "Lovecraftian" denoted the unique writing style found in his first story, *Dagon*, published in *The Vagrant* in 1919, and his last, *The Haunter of the Dark*, published in 1935.

It is imperative to note that the commercially successful *Ancient Aliens* was inspired by H.P. Lovecraft. Erich von Däniken, Graham Hancock, Dr. Morris Jessup, and Zecharia Sitchin are among those who drank deeply from the Lovecraftian well, skillfully plagiarizing his apocalyptic parables in a tribute of pseudoscience.

4

THE BRIDGE TO THE APOCALYPSE

Ancient religious and mythological texts have foretold that the paranormal is the hidden bridge to the Apocalypse, both steeped in arcane and forbidden knowledge. If this premise is correct, are these intertwined paradigms understandable—or do they lie beyond human comprehension?

Although the Greek word apokalypsis translates to "revelation" or "unveiling," it is usually associated with catastrophic events leading to the End of Days as wrought by God's judgment. It resonates with the moment the pleasures tasted in the Garden of Eden end, and we get on our knees in a final act of atonement. Some will engage in fanatical prayer and penance and give away their possessions to the poor. Others will gather in churches, in contrition, awaiting the return of the conquering King with heaven's armies at His side. The Bible describes the Second Coming in beautifully ambiguous prose —atop a white stallion, a warlord charges across the horizon. On his robe and on his thigh, he has a name that no one knows but he himself—king of kings and lord of lords. He is also called "Faithful and True" and the "Word of God." He has eyes of blazing fire, many crowns, and a sharp sword projecting from his mouth. His robe drips in blood. That description is recorded in Revelation 19:11-16:

> *I saw heaven standing open and there before me was a white horse, whose rider is called Faithful and True. With justice he judges and makes war. His eyes are like blazing fire, and on his head are many crowns. He has a name written on him that no one knows but he himself. He is dressed in a robe dipped in blood, and his name is the Word of God. The armies of heaven were following him, riding on white horses and dressed in fine linen, white and clean. Out of his mouth comes a sharp sword with which to strike down the nations. 'He will rule them with an iron scepter.' He treads the winepress of the fury of the wrath of God Almighty. On his robe and on his thigh, he has this name written: king of kings and lord of lords.*

Apocalyptic myths have always gripped our imagination, reflecting anxieties surrounding the Second Coming and end of civilization. As doomsday myths intertwine with the religious and paranormal, fear is the primordial glue that keeps them together. Fear is the most basic instinct and the mechanism that keeps us alive. It drives the proverbial train. You may argue the point, claiming that love, joy, and forgiveness are more important—and perhaps in a moral or philosophical sense they are—but it is fear that is our first response to the snake's stare and is the Law of the Jungle's supreme mandate. The required alchemy of fear meshes the paranormal with the apocalyptic, as H.P. Lovecraft's familiar albeit overused quote suggests:

> *The oldest and strongest emotion of humankind is fear, and the oldest and strongest kind of fear is fear of the unknown.*

With no tangible parameters, the paranormal is an amorphous blob encompassing time travel, remote viewing, mind control, altered states, parallel universes, and all the square pegs that fit into inexplicable and unbelievable circles. In the hurricane of white noise, shrill voices, and academic denial, wanderers roam onto isolated roads surrounded by detours and ideological fever swamps. The para-normal veers through unchartered territory, into tight, dark places, and over the Apocalypse's hidden bridge. The signposts can only be read by those who decipher the arcane signage—constant and unbroken stories spoken throughout history from primitive cave dwellings to Babylonian courtyards.

The Last Man on Earth featured Vincent Price as Dr. Robert Morgan, who is immune to the plague that has turned everyone else into a vampire. The science-fiction horror film was based on the Richard Matheson novel *I Am Legend* (1954.) Public domain.

Sadly, each generation arrogantly squanders these lessons—as George Santayana (1863–1952), Harvard University professor of philosophy, instructed with his aphorism, "Those who cannot remember the past are condemned to repeat it"—wasting opportunities to acknowledge ancestors and spirit guides, who, like smiling elves, give us a nod and point to our destiny. Many cross the bridge frightened and disconnected. Albert Einstein discerned that humans, although connected to the universe, view themselves as detached, with delusional thoughts and feeling of separation:

> *This delusion is a kind of prison for us, restricting us to our personal desires and to affection for a few persons nearest to us. Our task must be to free ourselves from this prison by widening our circle of compassion to embrace all living creatures and the whole of nature in its beauty.*

Einstein called it a "kind of optical delusion of (human) consciousness," leading to feelings of aloneness and despair. Hermann Karl Hesse (1877–1962) also addressed aloneness in *Steppenwolf* (1927), his novel exploring alienation and the search for meaning:

> *I am in truth the Steppenwolf that I often call myself; that beast astray who finds neither home nor joy nor nourishment in a world that is strange and incomprehensible to him.*

As Hesse struggled to understand his "strange and incomprehensible" world, he embraced a vital spiritual component, influenced by Carl Jung's psychoanalytic theories and Eastern mysticism and reincarnation. Hesse addressed the multidimensional nature of the soul and the notion that the individual is made up of countless selves—the transmigration of the soul into "thousands and thousands" of numerous identities—that can be rearranged in various ways, much like chess pieces. Hesse was awarded the Nobel Prize in Literature in 1946 for his significant contributions to literature, demonstrating unique insight into the human psyche and struggle with the duality of courage and fear.

Apocalyptical Monster

Fear of the apocalyptical monster conjures an ancestorial storm of fight, flight, freeze, or assimilation. It thrusts us into survival mode, protecting our cradled inner child. The awaited Apocalypse forces us to determine the reason for our suffering as we replace madness with consciousness. We cannot survive in an environment foretelling an apocalypse of pain and suffering—unless that suffering has an established natural order. We can understand if we are being punished for our wickedness and fall from grace, but if we are being made to suffer without reason nor provocation, then that realization can lead to madness, suicide, or messianic leaders who promise salvation in a cult paradise. For many, it's easier to follow the crowd and think like the crowd. Go along to get along! Not using rational thinking but sliding down into the slime of the lowest common denominator is safer. It's all part of the sheep mentality that fosters bland and rigid conformity and allegiance to widespread media propaganda.

We should question leaders and authority. As Greek philosopher Aristotle said, "Be a free thinker and don't accept everything you hear as truth. Be critical and evaluate what you believe in." But that mindset rarely happens with the easily influenced and imitative masses, who, as Johann Wolfgang von Goethe (1749–1832), the most influential writer in the German language, said cannot even comprehend what they want:

> *Nothing is more disgusting than the majority: because it consists of a few powerful predecessors, of rogues who adapt themselves, of weak who assimilate themselves, and the masses who imitate without knowing at all what they want.*

But knowing what we should do, with strength and courage, is different from roads traveled in fear and subjugation. Just look at the sad list of individuals who mindlessly followed cult leaders Jim Jones, Charles Manson, and Adolf Hitler, and the social dysfunction and violence that accompanied it. Before being sentenced to death on the gallows for his war crimes against humanity, Rudolf Höss confessed, "All I was doing was following the orders of my Führer!" Those sentiments were expressed by Höss, who had been appointed SS Commandant of the newly created Nazi Auschwitz-Birkenau extermination camp. Höss transformed the camp into the Nazis' central killing center, choosing Zyklon B as the most efficient method of gassing. As he later said, gassing was preferable to shooting because the latter:

> Would have placed too heavy a burden on the SS men who had to carry it out, especially because of the women and children among the victims.

As Auschwitz's longest-serving commandant, Höss was directly responsible for the killing of an estimated 1.1 million people and recognized for his loyalty to Hitler and cruelty to concentration camp prisoners. In her book *Political Tribes: Group Instinct and the Fate of Nations* (2019), Amy Chua noted:

> Humans are tribal. We need to belong to groups. We crave bonds and attachments, which is why we love clubs, teams, fraternities, and family. Almost no one is a hermit. Even monks and friars belong to orders.

Chua believes the tribal instinct forces us to belong, and that people will kill and die for ethnic, religious, sectarian, or clan-based group identities. Human response does not change over the centuries. Humans remain the same: predictably sad, eager to step in line, and, like Rudolf Höss, salute their masters, who offer us little, as observed by Erasmus, 1509:

The less talent they have, the more pride, vanity, and arrogance they have. All these fools, however, find other fools who applaud them.

Individuals who live meaningless and unfulfilled lives are often seduced into the vicelike allegiance of cult membership. These intellectually and spiritually vacant unfortunates are easily exploited in a complex array of psychological and sociological variables. Cult membership is a devil's bargain that destroys more than it offers. It: (1) trades autonomy for submission. (2) promises a new beginning and escape from one's dull and painful past. (3) barters away critical thinking, self-worth, and independence. (4) separates us from our community. (5) kills passion and creates a passive slave mentality. (6) revolts against civilization and gravitates towards a spartan and primitive lifestyle.

Philosopher Aldous Huxley (1894–1963), author of *Brave New World* (1932) and *The Doors of Perception* (1954), understood cult seduction as well:

People will come to love their oppression, to adore the technologies that undo their capacities to think.

That masochism is a variation of Stockholm syndrome, where the captive develops an attachment to the captor, transforming fear into "friendship." These positive feelings can apply to child abuse, coach-athlete abuse, relationship abuse, and sex trafficking but play only a small role in Huxley's despondent outlook. Huxley was a visionary harboring anxiety about the future. His *Brave New World* (1932) looked at the world through a dark lens, anticipating that in 2540, genetically engineered babies are produced on assembly lines, the social and economic divide between the rich and poor is legally enforced, and discontent is quelled by the mind control techniques of sex, entertainment, advertising, and mood-altering medications. Much like H. G. Wells (1866–1946), "The Father of Science Fiction,"

Huxley's prophecies have come to pass; in vitro fertilization, genetic cloning, transgender surgery, artificial intelligence, antidepressants, and stealth technology are common themes.

Irish poet Oscar Wilde (1854–1900) pessimistically remarked, "We are all in the gutter, but some of us are looking at the stars." In Albert Camus' *The Fall* (1956), former lawyer Jean-Baptiste Clamence dwells in that gutter, spending his days confessing moral failings to strangers in a dingy Amsterdam bar. He lives to express guilt and hope for redemption in personal Apocalypse, fearing the curse of monotony before death. Individuals like Clamence conclude that they are powerless; yet, in a final act of acceptance, they may choose to walk with a God of vengeance or a God of forgiveness.

The hidden bridge to the dreaded Apocalypse was depicted in the film *The Last Man on Earth* (1964), a post-apocalyptic film based on the novel *I Am Legend* (1954) by Richard Matheson, which explored the aftermath of a global plague. There is something of a gentle nuance that gives the film an other-worldly flavor with splendid pacing and an evolving story. It is now a cult favorite, as declared by Public Domain Movies:

> *Although the film was not considered a success upon its release, the film later gained a more favorable reputation as a classic of the genre. As of November 2011,* The Last Man on Earth *holds a 71% rating on Rotten Tomatoes. Phil Hall of Film Threat called* The Last Man on Earth *"the best Vincent Price movie ever made."*

In the plot, Dr. Robert Morgan exists in a world where infected humans turn into undead, vampiric creatures. The most significant moment is presented at the film's end, when Morgan retreats into a church and stands at the altar, denouncing his zombie pursuers as "freaks." He dies Christlike as he is impaled by a thrown spear. With his final breath, as his friend Ruth cradles him, he proudly declares that he is the last true man on Earth.

Morgan's death had purpose. It symbolized a bridge to the Apocalypse and a sacrificial message professing that he was a proud human being. Neurobiologists point out that humans share 98% of their DNA with chimpanzees, gorillas, and bonobos, but are separated from them by a unique 2% of DNA. That 2%, representing our cognitive, emotional, and spiritual selves, is the precious seed that Robert Morgan proclaimed as his rightful legacy, and something the rotting undead could never claim.

The similarities between humans and apes are amazing, such as: (1) the size of neurons. (2) The basic mechanism of channels and pumps that move sodium, potassium, and calcium around. (3) The neurotransmitters (serotonin, dopamine, glutamate) representing the same basic building blocks. But humans have more and have it better, and sometimes more is better. Addressing the "two percent solution," neuroscientist and primatologist Robert Sapolsky said the answer was shocking is its simplicity:

> *The main difference is in the sheer number of neurons. The human brain has 100 million times the number of neurons a sea slug's brain has. Where do those differences in quantity come from? At some point in their development, all embryos—whether human, chimp, rat, frog, or slug—must have a single first cell committed toward generating neurons. That cell divides and gives rise to 2 cells; those divide into 4, then 8, then 16. After a dozen rounds of cell division, you've got roughly enough neurons to run a slug. Go another 25 rounds or so and you've got a human brain. Stop a couple of rounds short of that and, at about one-third the size of a human brain, you've got one for a chimp.*

The difference is in the quantity which led to quality. Humans are vastly different because we have evolved and adapted better (not by climbing trees or swimming across an ocean) than any other species. We simply have more than they do, and Robert Morgan knew that.

The H.G. Wells novel *The Island of Dr. Moreau* (1896) is a convenient example. Wells is among the leading intellectuals and visionaries of all time. His groundbreaking science fiction novels, including *The Time Machine, The War of the Worlds,* and *The Invisible Man,* have stood the test of time and are considered classics in every sense. Erle C. Kenton's 1932 film adaptation of Wells' novel, *The Island of Lost Souls,* followed mad scientist Dr. Moreau performing operations on wild beasts to make them more human. When the beasts acted inappropriately, Moreau would crack his whip and challenge the beasts with the question "What is the law?" answered by the beasts and the Sayer of the Law:

> *Not to eat meat, that is the law. Are we not men?*
> *Not to go on all fours, that is the law. Are we not men?*
> *Not to spill blood, that is the law. Are we not men?*

"Are we not men?" is the same question Robert Morgan posed to the freaks.

We are born with inquisitiveness, the magic elixir of youth. It is what psychologist Daniel Berlyne called "epistemic curiosity," which he described as a drive aimed "not only at obtaining access to information-bearing stimulation, capable of dispelling uncertainties of the moment, but also at acquiring knowledge." He said it applied predominantly to humans, thus distinguishing the curiosity of humans from that of other species such as flesh-and-blood animals and paranormal "freaks."

Even though humans suffer from detachment, fear, and ignorance, the universe was built to be understandable. As indicated by Vedic, Buddhist, and Ancient Greek philosophies, these principles were intentionally woven into the fabric of reality, allowing for our comprehension. Einstein was in agreement as he asserted, "The eternal mystery of the world is its comprehensibility... The fact that it is comprehensible is a miracle."

Humans require a sense of order, a homeostasis assuring that the world operates within a system of understandable rules. And because we possess the capacity to realize and understand that order, like Robert Morgan, we are willing to sacrifice for it.

That is the law.

Question: You seem to be a fan of Vincent Prices' The Last Man on Earth. Can you tell us why?

5

NINETY SECONDS TO MIDNIGHT

I n the days before hand-written scrolls, movable type, and printing presses, news came to villages in the guise of wandering minstrels who entertained villagers with exaggerated stories of witches and trolls in parables of good and evil. In essence, it was fear as entertainment, a primitive invention that held sway over the super-stitious masses, bartering musical prophesy for food and ale. For centuries, charismatic prophets of doom, ordaining the end of the world, attracted rabid knowledge-starved followers.

One of their most enduring messages was the warning of God's wrath and certainty that the apocalypse was approaching. Retold in story and song, these epics of horror recounted the consequences of man's sins—Adam and Eve cast out of the Garden, the Great Flood, the Tower of Babel, the Destruction of Sodom and Gomorrah, the Testing of Job's Faith, the Four Horsemen of the Apocalypse.

And so, the people asked, "If this is the cursed message of yester-day, what will be the message of tomorrow?" Society harbors a fascination for the end-time prophesies of Christianity and Islam, by scientists, environmentalists, and military generals. These messages are all the same, differing only in subtle shades of despondency and a dim ringing of truth. Earth is being ravaged by pandemics, global warming, and wars in remote places most have never heard of. And, as we look at all of the swirling tea leaves, it appears that our planet is closer to cataclysm than previously thought.

The Doomsday Clock

Since 2023, the hands of the Doomsday Clock have remained at 90 seconds to midnight, reflecting the Bulletin of the Atomic Scientists' opinion about how much closer humankind has shifted toward global ruin. Writer Jon Kelvey views the Doomsday Clock as a metaphor, conceived not to end the threat of worldwide catastrophe, but as a means to generate discussion:

> *Initially conceived during the height of the Cold War as a way of signaling to policymakers and the public just how close nuclear brinkmanship was bringing the U.S. and Soviet Union to a disastrous nuclear war, the setting of the clock has more recently taken into account other potentially existential risks such as climate change and artificial intelligence.*

The Doomsday Clock was organized in 1945 at the dawn of the atomic era by Albert Einstein, J. Robert Oppenheimer, and University of Chicago scientists who had developed the Manhattan Project's atomic weapons. Forever known as the "father of the atomic bomb," Oppenheimer, feeling that he "had blood on his hands," later recalled Hindu scripture:

> *Now I am become Death, the destroyer of worlds.*

Oppenheimer's Doomsday Clock uses the imagery of apocalypse (midnight) and nuclear explosion (countdown to zero) to convey threats to humanity. The Doomsday Clock's message rests in the eye of the beholder. It has become an indicator of possible global catastrophe caused by man's neglect and abuse, or of random inexplicable events beyond our control.

Third Nuclear Age

The *Bulletin*'s Science and Security Board sets the Doomsday Clock every year after consulting with its Board of Sponsors, which includes nine Nobel laureates. Now the focus has shifted from their original concerns to threats of climate change and greenhouse gases. If the Clock's prophesy proves true, we are about to be thrown into the punishing fire, burning in the reality of nuclear war, environmental crisis, pandemics, and renegade technology. According to the clock, we are closer to midnight and closer to the end. Admiral Tony Radakin, the head of Britain's armed forces, warned that the world is standing on the cusp of a "third nuclear age" and threatened by coinciding challenges, weakened safeguards, and rogue states. He said:

> *Challenges include Russia's threat to use tactical nuclear weapons in Ukraine, China's drive to build up its nuclear stockpiles, Iran's failure to cooperate with international efforts to limit its nuclear program, and "erratic behavior" by North Korea.*

Radakin further explained that the dawning of a third nuclear age is defined by "multiple and concurrent dilemmas, proliferating nuclear and disruptive technologies, and the almost total absence of the security architectures that went before."

With all of the Doomsday Clock fearmongering about thermonuclear disaster, one would think the idea would be foremost on our minds. Strangely, it is not. What humans ultimately fear is the possibility that our world will be forever altered, and not for the better. That scenario lurks in many minds. In *The End of the World: Fear of the Apocalypse* (2019), Chapman University's Hannah Richardson observed:

The Chapman Survey of American Fears' data shows that only 16.4% of Americans are fearful of an apocalypse; while this number may seem low, there are a higher percentage of people who are afraid of the extinction of animals and plants, economic collapse, and warfare including nuclear and biological weapons ("America's Top Fears 2018" 2018). There is an overarching theme that people are fearful of everyday problems facing the world, and there is a fear that in the near future the world will never be the same.

Lovecraft was correct. We are more fearful of the unknown than of the here and now. A 2024 Ipsos Consumer Tracker asked Americans to select the scenario they feared the most from a list that included climate change, World War III, pandemics, total economic collapse, and killer robots. As reported by Christopher Good, the results were surprising:

The poll found that 33% of Americans feared economic collapse the most—beating out the runner-up, WWIII, by eight percentage points, and giving it a considerable lead on climate change (19%), another pandemic (12%), and killer robots (just 2%). Mark Fisher wrote that it's easier to imagine the end of the world than the end of capitalism, but the Americans we surveyed can imagine both.

The survey most likely reflected what is known as "accessibility bias," the human tendency to give more weight to information that comes to mind more easily—the economy as a classic example. Not only does it have a more direct impact on our lives than the other issues, but also a landslide of attention from the media, political campaigns, and even the marketing strategies of popular brands like Pringles Potato Chips, Nabisco Chips Ahoy, Capri Sun Fruit Punch, and Ritz Original Crackers, some now smaller in size and higher in cost. Consumers are extremely anxious about the economy despite drips and drabs of positivity in economic indicators that are dismissed or taken with a grain of salt.

Humans are creative and innovative. As we find ways to survive, we also find ways to destroy. The U.S. Census Bureau estimated that the world population increased by more than 71 million people in 2024 and would be 8.09 billion people on New Year's Day—representing 8.09 billion more ways to destroy our planet through disease, pollution, manmade disaster, and nuclear annelation.

The number of nuclear states, countries possessing nuclear weapons, has a terrifying history. In 1948, the Soviet Union detonated its first atomic bomb, and in 1985 Soviet leader Mikhail Gorbachev and U.S. President Ronald Reagan jointly declared that "a nuclear war cannot be won and must never be fought," a sentiment lasting for 37 years. But things turned in 2006 after North Korea conducted its first nuclear explosive test and withdrew from 2003 global treaty barring it from making nuclear weapons. And in 2018, President Trump withdrew from the Joint Comprehensive Plan of Action (JCPOA), which was signed in 2015 to place significant restrictions on the Islamic Republic of Iran's nuclear program. And again, in February 2022, after Russian President Vladimir Putin launched a full-scale invasion of Ukraine, the Kremlin chief used nuclear threats to intimidate other nations from intervening; then he abruptly suspended participation in New START, the last remaining nuclear weapons treaty.

The atomic bomb was intended to end Japan's military aggression, but while that objective was achieved, the danger, multiplied by global stockpiles, amassed through the Cold War and beyond, remains. Although it raised the specter of thermonuclear war and lobbied for saner nuclear policy, the Doomsday Clock was unable to achieve its goal of increasing awareness and worldwide nuclear disarmament.

According to the Federation of American Scientists, there are approximately 3,880 active nuclear warheads and 12,119 total nuclear warheads in the world as of 2024. The U.S. and Russia hold the vast majority of the world's nuclear weapons, with each possessing some 4,000 warheads.

Nuclear Little Ice Age

For the last four decades, scientists have run computer simulations to find out what the aftermath of nuclear war would look like. Atmospheric scientists Paul Crutzen and John Birks outlined a grim prophecy (1982) foreseeing that a nuclear war would produce a massive smoke cloud that would cause a "nuclear little ice age," blocking out sunlight and causing Earth's surface to become colder, dryer, and darker. Millions of people would be killed by blast waves and fires, devastating agriculture and civilization and leading to mass starvation worldwide. Radiation-induced cancers and genetic damage would affect the remaining population for generations.

There is always room for optimism, and it is always best to look upon what Ada Blenkhorn called the "sunny side of the street." In that regard, perhaps our only conceivable optimism is that, if the Doomsday Clock strikes midnight—perhaps 19 seconds from now—a new world order will emerge from the ashes. We still have time to ponder the probabilities of either punishment or redemption, and whether we will be greeted by doves of peace or pigeons from hell.

6

THE THOUSAND SCREAMS

Many apocalyptic beliefs are deeply rooted in esoteric mythology. The end of the world is not just prophesied, but woven into songs, stories, and ancient Hebrew, Egyptian, and Babylonian scriptures, as well as modern-day representations of Apocalyptic Awe. The Mesopotamian *Epic of Gilgamesh* and religious manuscripts are part of this tradition, attempting to understand the "incomprehensible unknown" and find meaning during chaotic times.

Breathing in the religious, philosophical, and paranormal, the Apocalypse is an essential part of our historical record. Although many believe these predictions are simply entertainment, the uncertainty they bring is undeniable. Some eschatologists are convinced they will experience the Apocalypse in their lifetime. The apocalyptical warning cry, "Humankind is doomed," has been drilled into our heads with a bombardment of messaging that is typically negative, tilting towards the catastrophic. Good news is often relegated to a single kernel of news, one small sliver of positivity and compassion.

But even though doomsday predictors have not agreed upon exact dates, they have forewarned that annihilation can occur at any time and in any manner. The Roulette Wheel of Death holds many possibilities, including global warming, coastal flooding, hurricanes, pandemics, terrorism, artificial intelligence, wars, genocide, and anything capable of rendering us cold and dead. But we have already been warned by the Four Horsemen of the Apocalypse and know what's coming! The following listing represents *specific* times when, throughout history, millions believed the world would end and they would be cast into the fire:

Nostradamus: The most famous of the prophets, the 16-century French astrologer and physician prophesied that the world would end in 3797.

1000: The year 1000 marked a significant point in Christian eschatology, as many believed it would herald the end of the world. This belief stemmed from interpretations of biblical prophecies and the widespread fear of the millennium. As the year approached, communities reacted with despondency and frenzied preparation. When the year passed without incident, the apocalyptic fervor subsided, but the psychological impact lingered, contributing to ongoing cycles of panic during subsequent millennia.

3797: Nostradamus (1503–1566): Possibly the most famous of the prophets, the 16th-century French astrologer and physician prophesied that the world would end in the year 3797. His book, *The Prophecies* (1555), contained cryptic quatrains credited with predicting historic events, from the French Revolution to the rise of Adolf Hitler, to the terrorist attacks of September 11, 2001, and even the 2020 coronavirus pandemic.

1666: The catastrophic Great Fire of London, mistaken as an apocalyptic sign, turned much of London into ashes. The blaze consumed over 13,000 houses, 87 churches, and left thousands of Londoners homeless.

17th century: Global explorer Christopher Columbus believed that the world would end in the 17th century.

1806: A hen belonging to fortune teller Mary Bateman, the Yorkshire Witch, began laying eggs on which the misspelled phrase "Crist is coming" was written. As news of this miracle spread, many people became convinced that doomsday had arrived

1815: The eruption of Mount Tambora was the largest volcanic eruption in recorded history and interpreted as heralding the end times. The eruption altered Earth's climate for years and led to the 1816 "Year Without Summer." Fast-moving lava initially killed around 10,000 people, while the aftermath altered the climate, blocked out the sun, and prevented crops from growing. This led to the deaths of an additional 80,000 people as it caused mass famine and disease, and smoke columns seen from over 300 miles away.

February 1835: The Mormon Armageddon. Joseph Smith, founder of the Mormon church, called a meeting of his church leaders to tell them that he had spoken to God and learned that Jesus would return within the next 56 years, after which, the End Times would begin.

April 23, 1843: Baptist farmer turned Christian Millerite leader William Miller (1843–1844) prophesized that the Second Coming of Christ would bring about the Last Judgement cleansing the world of sin and casting millions into hell. As the ill-fated date neared, Millerites sold all their possessions, donned white robes, and climbed to the tops of mountains to await their rapture into heaven. Scholars estimate that of some one million people who heard his message, about 100,000 chose to follow him.

October 1844: When nothing happened, Miller moved the date to October 1844, which also proved incorrect, leading some to label the non-event "The Great Disappointment." Most of the preacher's followers then abandoned him, some forming the Seventh-day Adventist Church.

1910: In 1881, an astronomer discovered that the tail of Haley's Comet contained the deadly cyanogen gas that Earth would pass through in 1910, leading to widespread panic.

1967: Rev. Jim Jones proclaimed that he had visions a nuclear attack would annihilate the country in 1967 and then relocated his People's Temple of the Disciples of Christ to South America to survive the holocaust.

1969: Charles Manson: The hippy cult leader predicted that "Helter Skelter," an apocalyptic race war, would occur in 1969. He used drugs, sex, persuasion, and the Bible to gain control of his cult followers.

1973: David Berg, the leader of the Children of God predicted that Comet Kohoutek, hurtling toward Earth at nearly 200,000 miles an hour and with a tail expected to stretch for 100 million miles, would bring about a colossal doomsday event. Berg's cult demonstrated at the United Nations building to warn about the "Christmas Monster."

1980s: In his book, *The 1980s: Countdown to Armageddon*, Hal Lindsey predicted that "the decade of the 1980s could very well be the last decade of history as we know it."

1982: In May 1980, televangelist and Christian Coalition founder Pat Robertson startled his *700 Club* TV show audience by claiming he knew when the world would end: "I guarantee you by the end of 1982 there is going to be a judgment on the world."

1982: UN official Mostafa Tolba, executive director of the UN Environment Program, warned:

> *By the turn of the century, an environmental catastrophe will witness devastation as complete, as irreversible, as any nuclear holocaust.*

1988: Followers of Hal Lindsey's *The Late Great Planet Earth* believed that the Tribulation (or Rapture) would occur no later than 1988. Lindsey suggested that Matthew 24:32-34 indicated that Jesus' return might be within "one generation" of Israel's rebirth and the rebuilding of the Jewish Temple.

1995: After the discovery of comet Hale-Bopp, expected to pass by Earth in 1997, the Heaven's Gate cult believed that an alien spacecraft was on its way to Earth, hidden from human detection because it was trailing the comet. The Heaven's gate website read:

> *Hale–Bopp brings closure to Heaven's Gate... Our 22 years of class-room here on planet Earth is finally coming to conclusion—'graduation' from the Human Evolutionary Level. We are happily prepared to leave 'this world.'*

1997: The bodies of 39 members of Heaven's Gate were found inside a Rancho Santa Fe, California mansion after committing suicide with a deadly cocktail of phenobarbital, apple sauce, and vodka. The techno-religious cult was founded in 1974 by Marshall Applewhite and Bonnie Nettles, who believed that aliens could provide them with a better place to live as they ascended to the Next Level. Kriti Mehrotra wrote:

> *All 39 Heaven's Gate cult members were dressed in identical black shirts and sweatpants, black-and-white Nike sneakers, and armband patches that read, "Heaven's Gate Away Team." They hoped that by ridding themselves of their 'containers' when the spacecraft was near Earth, they would be granted a new body by extraterrestrials, which would allow them to pass through Heaven's Gate and into a higher existence.*

December 31, 1999: Known as the Technological Apocalypse, the Millennium Bug, or the Y2K Virus, some believed that at midnight on December 31, 1999, a computer bug would crash the world's computer system, causing apocalyptic chaos on January 1, 2000. Society would cease to function, communications and travel would stop, and it would be the end of the world.

May 5, 2000: Richard Noone, author of the book *5/5/2000 Ice: the Ultimate Disaster* (1997), claimed that the Antarctic ice mass would be three miles thick by May 5, 2000—a date in which the planets would be aligned in the heavens, resulting in a global icy death.

2000: Edgar Cayce: The sleeping prophet predicted that the Second Coming would occur in 2000, in the same year Atlantis would rise.

2000: Noel Brown, director of the New York office of the UN Environment Program, said entire nations could be wiped off the face of the Earth by rising sea levels if the global warming trend is not reversed by the year 2000:

> *Shifting climate patterns would bring back 1930s Dust Bowl conditions to Canadian and U.S. wheatlands.*

April 6, 2005: Cult leader Warren Jeffs warned that the world would end on April 6, which is the day in 1830 when Joseph Smith founded the Church of Jesus Christ of Latter-day Saints. Some LDS leaders have also claimed it is Christ's true birthday.

June 12, 2008: Yisrayl "Buffalo Bill" Hawkins, founder of the House of Yahweh religious sect, predicted (incorrectly) the end of the world.

2008: According to God's Church minister Ronald Weinland, who called himself the "End-Time Prophet of God," the end times are upon us. His book *2008: God's Final Witness* (2006), revealed that hundreds of millions of people would die, and by the end of 2006:

> *There will be a maximum time of two years remaining before the world will be plunged into the worst time of all human history. By the fall of 2008, the United States will have collapsed as a world power and no longer exist as an independent nation.*

2008: Christian pastor Mark Biltz predicted the second coming of Jesus, preaching that the seven years of great tribulation would begin in the fall of 2008 and continue until the fall of the year 2015, when Jesus would come.

2010–2016: The blind Bulgarian mystic, Baba Vanga, predicted nuclear war between 2010 and 2016 would lead to the abandonment of Europe.

2010: Conspiracy theorist Alex Jones predicted that the release of the movie *Machete* (2010), an American exploitation action film directed by Robert Rodriguez and Ethan Maniquis, depicting Mexican illegals who triumph over the border vigilantes, would prompt a race war. Jones also incorrectly predicted terror attacks on April 15 or 19, 2010.

May 21, 2011: Harold Camping, a radio preacher from California, predicted the Rapture in 2011:

> *May 21st, there's going to be a terrific earthquake. Way bigger than anything the Earth has ever experienced, and that'll be the beginning of Judgment Day.*

When it failed to materialize, Camping changed the date to Oct. 21, 2011—the backup date for his predictions.

2011: Conspiracy theorist Alex Jones predicted the apocalyptical collapse of at least 15 European nations by the end of the year.

2012: Conspiracy theorist turned doomsday prophet, Alex Jones, predicted the devaluation of the U.S. dollar by 50% by 2012.

December 21, 2012: The Mayan calendar prophecy gained international attention, with many predicting it would signify the conclusion of a 5,126-year-long cycle and the end of the world. Various interpretations suggested that the Mayans had foreseen apocalyptic events due to the calendar's cyclical nature. While some embraced the notion of impending doom, others dismissed it as a misinterpretation of Mayan culture.

2014: Christian pastors Mark Blitz and John Hagee warned of the Blood Moon Prophecy—a series of four lunar eclipses (referred to as tetrads and coinciding with Jewish holidays) as signs of the end times.

September 28, 2015: Evangelical leader John Hagee predicted that a rare astronomical event called a "tetrad"—four consecutive and complete lunar eclipses (or blood moons)—would signal the Rapture's arrival.

2015: Christian pastor Mark Biltz predicted the second coming of Jesus, stating that the seven years of great tribulation would begin in the fall of 2008 and extend until the return of Jesus in 2015.

October 7, 2015: Chris McCann, eBible Fellowship founder, predicted the world would end in 2015, during a rising blood moon and supermoon.

2016: While promoting his movie, *An Inconvenient Truth* (2006), Al Gore said humanity had only 10 years left before the world would reach a point of no return. Gore's film also featured animations of water inundating Manhattan and Florida.

2018: Riley Stephenson, an obscure end times prophet, predicted that the Rapture would occur between March and May of that year. Even before May had fully passed, he revised the date to "Summer of 2020."

July 27, 2018: Internet pastor Paul Begley warned his YouTube followers that the super blood moon eclipse was a sign of the impending apocalypse. The alarmist used his video, Blood Moon Rising, to warn that God spoke to him of the Four Horsemen and the End of Days.

June 9, 2019: The Church of God's Ronald Weinland continually repeated that the world would end in 2011, 2012, 2013, and 2019.

2020: In 1971 Jeane Dixon, American astrologer, clairvoyant, and psychic, predicted that Armageddon would begin in 2020, during a world war, and that the world would end between 2020 and 2035.

2130: Baba Venga predicted aliens would help civilization live underwater by 2130 and that Earth would declare war against Mars in 3005.

December 22, 2032: Dubbed 2024 YR4 or the "Christmas Surprise," astronomers detected a space rock, an estimated 200 feet in length, that has a 1.3% probability of striking Earth. According to writer Victor Tangermann:

> 2024 YT4 comes in at a three on the Torino Impact Hazard scale, which measures the probability of an asteroid striking the Earth. A three, according to NASA's Jet Propulsion Lab, means that it's an "encounter, meriting attention by astronomers," plus attention by public and by public officials is merited if the encounter is less than a decade away.

Question: Chapter 6 is one of your most fascinating. What is The Thousand Screams all about?

2037: In 1971, Jeane Dixon, American astrologer, clairvoyant, and psychic, predicted the end times and Jesus' Second Coming in 2020 and also in 2037.

2037: Rep. Alexandria Ocasio-Cortez, while selling her "Green New Deal," said in 2025 that the world will end in 12 years if nothing is done to address climate change.

2043: Baba Vanga warned that Muslims would invade Europe in a "great Muslim war," which would end with the establishment of an Islamic caliphate by 2043, with Rome as its epicenter.

5079: Bulgarian blind mystic Baba Vanga predicted the end of the world.

7

APOCALYPTIC AWE

P rophesies have been envisioned and articulated—not by theologians or scientists, but by dreamers with the unique ability to peer beyond the veil into tomorrow's light. Using curiosity to channel future truths are legendary figures H.G. Wells, George Orwell, and Jules Verne. Yet, few readers have heard of Morgan Andrew Robertson, a visionary who seamlessly blended fiction with uncanny prophecy. According to the website *Interesting Literature*:

> *Although he overstated his role in predicting periscopic technology, Morgan Robertson* did *have an uncanny ability to foresee something even more momentous in 20th-century marine history.*

Robertson's novella, *Futility* (1898), described a fictional American ocean liner named *Titan* that sinks in the North Atlantic Ocean. After the *Titanic's* sinking on April 14, 1912, Robertson was credited with precognition. His story was uncanny in the accuracy of its details and its foretelling of *Titanic's* fate: (1) Both the *Titan* and *Titanic* sank after striking icebergs. (2) Neither had adequate lifeboats. (3) Both were considered unsinkable. (4) The fictitious *Titan* was 800 feet long. The *Titanic* was 882 feet long. (5) Both events took place in April. Robertson's novella was revised as *The Wreck of the Titan* in 1912, and just three years after the event he had eerily predicted took place, he died.

Jonathan Swift's name needs to be on that list as well. His book, *Gulliver's Travels* (1726), predicted the existence of two unknown satellites of Mars, which he called "Phobos" and "Deimos," predicting their discovery 150 years prior:

> *When the two Martian moons, Phobos and Deimos, were eventually found, by Asaph Hall at the U.S. Naval Observatory, their orbits proved to be quite similar to those described in Swift's novel. Phobos is actually 6,000 kilometers from the surface of Mars and revolves around Mars in 7.7 hours, whereas Swift gave the values 13,600 kilometers and 10 hours, respectively. Deimos averages 20,100 kilometers from Mars and orbits in 30.3 hours; Swift gives 27,200 kilometers and 21.5 hours, respectively.*

Paranormal cult literature has questioned how Swift knew about the Martian moons, with one outrageous possibility being that he himself was a Martian. Irrespective of how Swift is perceived, the fact remains that both Swift and Robertson were born with a burning curiosity to know things of the unknown.

Therapeutic Salve

The Book of Revelation has portrayed end times with boils on our flesh, waters turning to blood, drought, darkness, and natural catastrophes. If this is how it ends for the 8 billion humans who live on the planet, then Apocalyptic Awe may offer a therapeutic salve granting us a glance at plagues and floods from a different perspective, one providing solace, healing, and positive distraction. With the ability to adapt and survive, humans have turned madness into exquisite Apocalyptic Awe—embracing the end times through popular films, books, and music. In what portends to be the start of an end times trilogy, director Danny Boyle's 2002 dystopian thriller *28*

Days Later focused on two apocalyptic trends: global pandemic and undead zombies, who were actually infected humans. His sequel, *28 Years Later* (2025), introduced slothful zombies called "Slow-Lows," who crawl around scavenging for worms. *28 Days Later: The Bone Temple* represents the third installment of Apocalyptic Awe attraction, infection, and rage.

At the juncture where fascination replaces fear, the premise of Apocalyptic Awe magically takes shape. Consider the massive mushroom clouds rising over Las Vegas, resulting from above-ground nuclear blasts. Climbing majestically into the skies, those clouds were accompanied by hundreds of nuclear tests performed underground between 1951 and 1992 in the desert, 65 miles outside the city's glitz and glitter. Oddly, these ugly radiation-spewing weapons captured the public's imagination throughout the 1950s and early 1960s and became a promotional tool called "nuclear tourism." The Vegas Chamber of Commerce promoted the dates and times of these tests so tourists could enjoy the spectacle of a mushroom cloud. Bomb-watching became the rage. Thrill-seeking tourists tried to get the closest spot possible to ground zero. On the eve of detonations, Las Vegas businesses would organize "Dawn Bomb" parties. Beginning at midnight, guests would drink and sing until the flash of the bomb lit up the night sky. Sin City promoters recruited the Sands Hotel's lead dancer to symbolize Las Vegas' fantasy and spectacle. The poster gal wore a fluffy mushroom cloud-shaped swimsuit with bombs in the background. Bedtime stories, biblical parables, and popular myths reflect the Apocalyptic Awe, with perhaps the best example found in Hal Lindsey's *The Late, Great Planet Earth* (1970), which, combining religious doom with secular fear, sold over 28 million copies. Eschatological "theologians" like Lindsey focus on the trials and tribulations of the end times. It offers enlightenment in the form of entertainment, exploring the dark side—not in fear, but in awe and fascination—the very concept of Apocalyptic Awe. To be clear, we use fear to create art as a means of understanding that which we fear. Consider that one widespread fear among white America is of the Black drug dealer who wants to drag us into the back alley, get us hooked, and then rape our women—another variation of the Mandingo sexual archetype.

Those racist fears took shape as a specific type of motion picture, all reiterating ugly stereotypes and misconceptions. During the early-1970s, films about Black drug dealers, addicts, and pimps were in vogue, despite outcries from social reformers criticizing the genre for stereotyping Black Americans. Labeled "blaxploitation," 10 of the most representative include: (1) *Cotton Comes to Harlem* (1970). Director: Ossie Davis. (2) *Shaft* (1971), Director: Gordon Parks. (3) *Superfly* (1972), Director: Gordon Parks, Jr. (4) *Across 110th Street* (1972). Director: Barry Shear. (5) *Trouble Man* (1972), Director: Ivan Dixon. (6) *Slaughter's Big Rip-Off* (1973), Director: Gordon Douglas. (7) *Black Caesar* (1973), Director: Larry Cohen. (8) *The Mack* (1973), Director: Michael Campus. (9) *Foxy Brown* (1974), Director: Jack Hill. (10) *Friday Foster* (1975), Director: Arthur Marks.

Typically shot on shoe-string budgets, they examined a slice of Black culture within a needle-ridden urban wasteland. Later, director Spike Lee's term "Magical Negro" expressed his anger, after Hollywood exploited the stereotype of a "magical Black character" who possesses mystical powers and selflessly helps white protagonists, as in *The Green Mile* (1999) and *The Legend of Bagger Vance* (2000).

Decades later, those outcries went unheard, after Hollywood exploited, not *Little Black Sambo* or *Amos 'n' Andy*, but environmental horrors. This genre of environmental apocalypse, echoing admonitions that disasters were caused by the wrath of God, brought about several unexpected outcomes: (1) Our fascination with environmental destruction was titillated. (2) Therapy, in the guise of positive distraction, was combined with entertainment. (3) Human resilience and survival were celebrated. (4) Destruction and renewal became popular morality plays. (5) Disaster movies proved profitable at the box office.

Consider the genre of commercially successful and notable disaster films that have entertained us for over 50 years: (1) *Snowpiercer* (2013), Director: Bong Joon-ho. (2) *Noah* (2014), Director: Darren Aronofsky. (3) *Melancholia* (2011), Director: Lars von Trier. (4) *The Day After Tomorrow* (2004), Director: Roland Emmerich. (5) *The Perfect Storm* (2000), Director: Wolfgang Petersen. (6) *The Ice Storm* (1997), Directors: Ang Lee, Ronald Neame. (7) *Waterworld* (1995), Director: Kevin Reynolds. (8) *Twister* (1996), Director: Jan de Bont. (9) *The Poseidon Adventure* (1972), Directors: Irwin Allen, Ronald Neame.

One of the most popular of the genre was the "apocalyptic action film" *The Day After Tomorrow* (2004), depicting a group struggling to survive tornadoes, tidal waves, and earthquakes, all plunging the planet into a new ice age. The film was based on *The Coming Global Superstorm* (1999) by Art Bell and Whitley Strieber. *Day After* premiered in Mexico City and made $552 million worldwide, becoming the sixth-highest-grossing film of the year.

Undead zombies warned us of the danger of pandemics and bioterrorism. *Night of the Living Dead* (1968), *The Walking Dead* (2010), and *World War Z* (2013) gave shape and substance to those fears, while the apocalyptic films *Mad Max* (1979), *The Road* (2009), and *Children of Men* (2006) provide hope that somehow humans will survive.

Another glimpse into our dystopian future came from director Christopher Nolan in *Interstellar* (2014). Suffering a blight, like the 1930s Dust Bowl, a devastated 21st century suffers a catastrophic crop-destroying pathogen. Nolan, drawing from a unique palette of styles, has directed some of the most thought-provoking movies, including *Inception, Memento,* and *The Dark Knight Trilogy*. With no connections in the film industry, his signature films have grossed more than $5 billion worldwide, allowing him to see "the crooked inner world inside the character's head."

Nolan is no stranger to apocalyptical themes, having written and directed *Oppenheimer* (2023), the account of American theoretical physicist J. Robert Oppenheimer, who tested the first nuclear weapon and helped create the Doomsday Clock. Writer Polina Pompliano observed that self-taught writer and film director Nolan didn't go to film school, nor did he ever study film in a formal way, "yet he's arguably one of the best living directors in the world." Strikingly, one of Nolan's most quotable quotes pertained to optimism during the end days, told in a direct, simplistic tone:

A hero can be anyone, even a man doing something as simple and reassuring as putting a coat on a young boy's shoulders to let him know the world hadn't ended.

Pink Sidewalks and Existential Dread

The specter of climate change has led to worry about environmental disaster and an impending Armageddon, especially for individuals living on vulnerable fault lines and on low-level seacoasts. Some espouse environmental ideas by anthropomorphizing Mother Earth, who is punishing us for disrespecting nature. Although the warning is often challenged or ignored, the major cause of natural disasters is climate change. The facts are (this writer believes) irrefutable— icebergs are melting and oceans are rising, while coal-burning factories pollute the planet, leading to increased hurricanes and forest fires.

One artist has successfully blended all those anxieties into an alchemy of pink sidewalks and existential dread. "This is all pink and attractive, but we are going to die," was engraved into the exhibition by Anastasia Samoylova. The Russian-born American photographer garnered critical acclaim for her controversial yet subtle images of Florida's collapsing pastel-pink landscapes. Samoylova was inspired by the disparity between the state's severe weather events and its aging infrastructure. Her exhibition *Flood Zone* (2019) was a surreal chronicle of an area decaying in real time and a portent of Hurricane Milton, the Category 3 storm, and the third hurricane after Debbie and Helene, to make landfall in Florida in 2024. Samoylova:

Everything is intertwined. That's why I think isolating climate change as something detached and abstract, and visually associated with melting ice caps, is very dangerous because we're in the moment right now. Every political decision is going to affect us on this daily basis.

Samoylova's art is a romantically colorized version of Apocalyptic Awe, with bubblegum-colored concrete, flooded swimming pools, uprooted palm trees, and displaced alligators. She renders a post-apocalyptic picture of urban decay, excessive heat waves, and historic flooding, turning one person's misery into another's art.

If we allow fear to consume us, we will be trapped in crippling hyper-vigilance, awaiting the next real or imagined catastrophe. Ripping our flesh and dying like dogs, our minds will be destroyed by relentless anxiety. But, for fear to be tamed, it must be transformed. Literary prophets like Fyodor Dostoevsky, Anthony Burgess, Kurt Vonnegut Jr., and James Graham Ballard were essential architects of that transformative positive distraction. Like Jung and Freud's "talk therapy," looking at fear through another lens helps to control it with defined and less-fearful parameters.

Ballard (1930–2009) moved beyond science-fiction's redundancy of the 1930s–1950s, inviting us into a forbidden dystopian realm. He believed Earth was the only truly alien planet and that science-fiction was not about outer space, but about the inner space of human psychopathology. In *The Drowned World* (1962), individuals experience strange dreams that regress them to primitive times. *The Drowned World* depicts a post-apocalyptic Earth, ravaged by floods spawned by melted ice caps and solar radiation. Ballard imagined London as a tropical swamp infested with giant iguanas, albino alligators, and endless swarms of malarial insects, all caused by climate change. His disaster trilogy included *The Drowned World* (1962), *The Draught* (1965), and *The Crystal World* (1966).

Ballard's surreal intuition was the result of real-life experiences suffered by fellow authors, including Fyodor Dostoevsky (1821–1881), Anthony Burgess (1917–1993), and Kurt Vonnegut Jr. (1922–2007). Ballard was born in Shanghai of English parents and, at age ten, was incarcerated in the Lunghua concentration camp by the Japanese occupiers, from 1943 to 1945, as recounted in *Empire of the Sun*.

Anthony Burgess' *A Clockwork Orange* (1962) was not inspired by some nocturnal nightmare fantasy, but by witnessing the actual attack and beating of his first wife Lynne. The attack by a gang of drunk American servicemen stationed in England during World War II stirred him to channel his grief and rage into one of the best illustrations of dystopian satire. At that time, England was gripped by fear over juvenile delinquency and a developing youth culture based around coffee bars, rock music, and violent, leather-clad, chain-wielding Teddy Boys. Irving Schulman's novel *The Amboy Dukes* (1946) explored a similar theme.

Dostoevsky was sent to debtors' prison, where he wrote *Notes from the House of the Dead* (1864), a sober tale of prison life. Later, *Crime and Punishment* (1866) and *The Brothers Karamazov* (1880) explored the depths of human psychology, where good and evil trespassed in the dead of night. Romanticized as a tortured genius, the poet, orphan, and gambler was imprisoned for participating in a literary group critical of the Czar. Dostoevsky was blindfolded and placed in front of a firing squad. But seconds before the triggers were pulled, he was acquitted and sent to a Siberian prison camp.

Kurt Vonnegut's book *Slaughterhouse-Five* (1969) looked back upon his horrific ordeal as a prisoner of war in a Dresden prison camp. Vonnegut, whose 106th Infantry Division fought in the Battle of the Bulge, was among the 50 American soldiers captured by the Germans. Vonnegut lived in an underground slaughterhouse, where he survived the Allied firebombing of February 13–15, 1945. Vonnegut, a master of morbid humor, blends elements of technology and religion through a sarcastic lens. His fictitious book, *The Day the World*

Ended, not to be confused with either the 1955 or 2001 films of the same name, was included in Vonnegut's science fiction fantasy, *Cat's Cradle* (1963), describing what people were doing on the day Dresden was bombed.

Although truth is believed to be the province of priests and shamans, curiosity provides us with the key to unlock the door. Philosopher and psychologist William James (1842–1910) called curiosity "the impulse towards better cognition," meaning the desire to explore and comprehend the unknown. He noted that, in children, it drives them towards objects of novel, sensational qualities—that which is "bright, vivid, startling." Curiosity is the driving force behind our need to unlock the secrets of the paranormal. Curiosity is the magical elixir of youth that allows us to create our personalized science fiction and peer into tomorrow's ether.

Fear and curiosity go together like peanut butter and jelly. As with children and animals, we share fear and curiosity in equal measure. The moth to the flame. The rat to the cheese. The spider watching the fly. Fear captivates us, mesmerizes us, and attracts us, while literature, music, and film breathe life into Apocalyptic Awe, helping us control the beast through art.

As an example, both Erich von Däniken's pseudoscience and Hal Lindsey's eschatology tapped into an unexpected zeitgeist curiosity. The single most important element of their uncanny success was the repackaging of esoteric information in an entertaining and somewhat easy-to-understand manner that satisfied our need to know about ancient and forthcoming events. It was curiosity, not faith, love, or fear, that propelled those authors to the top of the million-dollar food chain.

Like many of my generation, classic 1950s science-fiction and fantasy inspired me. The imagery of H.G. Wells, Jules Verne, Robert Louis Stevenson, Edgar Allen Poe, and George Orwell; much later, Ray Bradbury, Stephen King, and Dean R. Koontz drew me in. I knew that somewhere in those books, I could find the answer. If I could read enough of their words, I could discover secrets that had eluded others. That curiosity was the driving force that led me to the pathway.

But, of all those voices and words, H.P. Lovecraft said it best, in his dry, academic tone, skillfully setting up his horrible visions of fear and incomprehension. All the other writers looked for answers that Lovecraft knew could not be found. The answers are unknowable, and that is the real horror of the paranormal. Fascinated by Lovecraft's vision, I attempted to develop it further. Conceptually, I write about pain and suffering and hope and redemption. I explore fear and trauma, recognizing that many of us, perhaps all of us, suffer the pain of misery and aloneness. I believe that we are all flawed; but we can all be fixed. To that end, I explore dark themes as a way of understanding and taming what Lovecraft called the "Crawling Chaos" and what I call the Apocalyptic Awe.

Question: You have coined the term "Apocalyptic Awe," a combination of fear and curiosity that seems to define the research in your book. Can you describe what this means?

8

THE MASQUE OF THE RED DEATH

And so many died that all believed that it was the end of the world.

— AGNOLO DI TURA DEL GRASSO, THE SCRIBE OF
THE BLACK DEATH

Agnolo di Tura del Grasso's apocalyptic omen was reflected in Edgar Allen Poe's *The Masque of the Red Death* (1842), which warned there would be no escape from the plague's "Darkness and Decay." In Poe's story, a disease known as the Red Death causes its victims to die quickly and gruesomely, with seizures and bleeding from the pores. However, Prince Prospero, who is wealthy and powerful, feels he can avoid infection and cheat death. He gathers a thousand of his knights and dames into his palace for a masquerade ball and welds the gates shut to keep out the disease.

Still, at the stroke of midnight, a ghoulish stranger appears in garments resembling a funeral shroud with a corpse-like mask. Prophetically, Prospero and his guests die, as Poe concludes that death and disease are inevitable, having "dominion" over the mere mortals who profess to defy them.

Historically, Poe had much to draw upon, in particular the Black Death, a pandemic caused by the bubonic plague—*Yersinia pestis*—that devastated Europe and Asia in the mid-1300s. It is believed to have arrived in October 1347, when 12 ships from the Black Sea docked at the Sicilian port of Messina. It was *Danse Macabre*—the dance of death. As the plague spread, rodents, cats, and rats died, causing fleas to seek other blood sources. Unsuspecting sailors, living in filthy, cramped quarters, were infected by flea bites, plague bacteria, or cough droplets. Most of them died.

Sicilian authorities ordered the "death ships" out of the harbor, but the contagion had already been let loose. Over the next five years, the Black Death would kill more than 20 million people in Europe—almost a third of the continent's population. Like Poe's Red Death, the symptoms of the Black Death were horrendous, as Italian poet Giovanni Boccaccio, most famously known for *The Decameron*, described:

> *In men and women alike, at the beginning of the malady, certain swellings, either on the groin or under the armpit, waxed to the bigness of a common apple, others to the size of an egg, some more and some less, and these the vulgar named plague-boils.*

In Siena, Italy, half the population of 60,000 died, as described by Agnolo di Tura del Grasso. In *Plague in Siena: An Italian Chronicle* (1349), he said that "those who did not see such horribleness can be called blessed," describing the plague as so awful that it was impossible to recount—writing:

> *And the victims died almost immediately. They would swell beneath their armpits and in their groins and fall over dead while talking. Father abandoned child, wife husband, one brother a brother; for this illness seemed to strike through the breath and sight. And so, they died. And none could be found to bury the dead for money or friendship. Members of a household brought their*

dead to a ditch as best they could, without priest, without divine offices. Nor did the death bell sound. And in many places in Siena great pits were dug and piled deep with the multitude of dead. And they died by the hundreds both day and night, and all were thrown in those ditches and covered over with earth. And as soon as those ditches were filled more were dug.

Known to the commoners as the Black Death, the bubonic plague attacked the lymphatic system, causing horrible swelling in the lymph nodes. Blood and pus seeped out. Then followed fever, chills, vomiting, diarrhea, terrible aches and pains, and death—like in Poe's apocalyptic horror. The stage has already been set. If we were able to peer into some mythical crystal ball, we would see the next plague staring back. Agnolo di Tura del Grasso, the Black Death's scribe, concluded "And so many died that all believed that it was the end of the world."

And for some, that is true. Blood continually spills in remote locales, rarely reaching the front pages of our newspapers and websites. Presently (2023), there are 15 armed conflicts encompassing both government forces and armed non-state rebels smoldering in remote places, including Cameroon, Ethiopia, Mozambique, Mali, Burkina Faso, South Sudan, and the Democratic Republic of Congo, hampering public health efforts to thwart emerging pandemics. The wonders of globalization, connecting the modern world to remote deserts and jungles, is a two-sided sword. Globalization has accelerated the spread of pathological agents, resulting in worldwide pandemics. A *Brazilian Journal of Psychiatry* paper, *Pandemic Fear and COVID-19: Mental Health Burden and Strategies*, identified the increased health challenges:

This has added greater complexity to the containment of infections, which has had an important political, economic, and psychosocial impact, leading to urgent public health challenges. HIV, Ebola, Zika, and H1N1, among other diseases, are recent examples.

Health officials continuously monitor genetic mutations that could spawn dangerous human-to-human contagions. One of the most concerning facts about viruses, particularly those of the coronavirus family, is their ability to rapidly mutate, allowing the virus to better bind to receptors in the upper airways of humans. New strains of bird flu have caused hundreds of deaths over the years, mainly through exposure to infected animals. H7N9 (considered the influenza A virus with the greatest potential public health impact) and H5N1 are the most likely strains to infect humans.

A global outbreak of mpox (monkeypox) was detected in 2022 and, in 2024, British health officials identified four cases of a more infectious version of mpox that first emerged in the Democratic Republic of the Congo. This was the first time the variant caused illness outside Africa. Mpox is a viral illness affected by the monkeypox virus, a species of the genus *Orthopoxvirus*. Common symptoms of mpox are a skin rash or mucosal lesions, which can last 2–4 weeks, accompanied by fever, headache, muscle aches, back pain, low energy, and swollen lymph nodes. Mpox can be transmitted through close contact with someone who has mpox, with contaminated materials, or with infected animals.

Virologists have identified education, isolation, and inoculation as the most effective ways to contain and destroy natures microscopic madness and plagues like the Ebola virus and Lassa Fever. Added to the challenges has been the weaponization of Covid-19 during the 2020–2021 outbreak, with one group promoting vaccinations and mask wearing and another arguing that their individual freedoms are more important than compliance.

Recent pandemics, accounting for millions of deaths in both modern-day cities and remote tropical jungles, are listed in the following tally, as though the rat-infested ships have returned with the Black Plague's cargo and a grinning Prince Prospero at the helm.

9

THE PANDEMICS

I n past times, when the sun was blotted out by darkened skies, those who witnessed an eclipse interpreted it as a portent of impending doom. A similar celestial event occurred on April 8, 2024, when 40 million people in Canada, Mexico, and the United States experienced a total solar eclipse when the moon darkened the midday sun.

For most, this modern-day eclipse was an easily explained scientific phenomenon. But others, always looking for signs, claimed it represented a systematic pattern and a timeline of approximately one decade before another plague would be unleashed. Can this happen again? Are we prepared for another pandemic?

Science has eradicated many of nature's deadly aberrations with remarkable victories: (1) Edward Jenner created the first effective vaccine to eradicate the smallpox virus, which killed an estimated 300 million people in the 20th century. (2) Rinderpest, a viral disease that infected cattle and other mammals, has been successfully eradicated. (3) Polio has been virtually eliminated worldwide. Although still diagnosed, the lowest annual prevalence of wild Polio (22 cases) was in 2017. (4) Dracunculiasis, a parasite in contaminated drinking water, is the cause of Guinea worm disease. In 2017, the global annual incidents of the disease had been reduced to 30 cases, down from 3.5 million in 1986. (5) Malaria, spread through bites from infected female Anopheles mosquitos, has been eradicated from most parts of the world. The global mortality rate fell by 60% between 2000 and 2015 and is expected to be eliminated by 2040. (6) Diphtheria, once a leading cause of death for children, is a contagious airborne disease caused by toxin-producing bacteria that spreads from person to person after an infected person coughs or sneezes. The vaccine used to treat it was developed in 1923 and now the disease is exceedingly rare in the U.S.

Vigilance is key. It's crucial that we contain occult diseases before they mutate out of our control, perhaps learning valuable lessons from earlier human suffering:

541: The first reported pandemic (*Yersinia pestis*), designated the Plague of Justinian (541–542 CE), broke out in Egypt and became one of the most devastating pandemics in history, claiming millions of lives and causing widespread societal upheaval across the Byzantine Empire. The plague was carried by black rats (*Rattus rattus*) traveling on grain ships and arriving in Constantinople in 542 CE. It continued to spread throughout the Mediterranean world for another 225 years, finally disappearing in 750 CE.

1346–1353: The Bubonic Plague ravaged Europe and the Mediterranean region, killing over 50 million people—more than 60% of Europe's entire population. The plague was mainly spread through the bite of a flea infected with the plague-causing bacterium, *Yersinia pestis*. Humans, bit by fleas, exhibited within three to five days, fever, headache, chills, and fatigue. Without prompt antibiotic treatment, 30% to 100% of infected people die.

1878: The Avian influenza, or "fowl plague," was first recorded in Italy, but it took until 1955 to discover that the virus causing bird flu was a type A influenza virus, described as a contagious disease of poultry and associated with high mortality. Avian influenza A viruses are classified into two categories: highly pathogenic avian influenza (HPAI) and low pathogenic avian influenza (LPAI.)

1894: The bubonic plague of 1894 was the first major outbreak encountered by the Hong Kong government. Two months after the discovery of the first patient, the death toll rose to 2,442, accounting for over 10% of the total population. It represented Hong Kong's first and deadliest epidemic, and, on May 10, the city was declared an infected port, from which Chinese locals were prohibited to depart the territory.

1918–1919: The Spanish Flu (the Spanish Lady) is believed to have caused between 25 million and 50 million deaths.

1918: What were believed to be the first confirmed U.S. cases of a deadly global flu pandemic were reported among U.S. Army soldiers stationed at Fort Riley, Kansas; 46 soldiers would die. (The influenza outbreak would ultimately kill an estimated 20 million to 40 million people worldwide.) Note: The two most severe and common flu strains are Flu A, which can infect both humans and animals, and Flu B, which only infects humans, changes more slowly, and tends to be milder. The 1918 flu pandemic was caused by Flu A, which is generally more severe than Flu B.

1957: The 1957 pandemic flu virus, or influenza, caused an estimated one million to two million deaths worldwide.

Mid-1960s: HIV-1(subtype B) successfully emerged out of Africa and took hold in the Caribbean by 1967. A Haitian HIV strain from 1969 is the closest relative to those that first dropped into New York, suggesting it may have been the source of America's outbreak. The virus was also circulating among Haiti, the Dominican Republic, Jamaica, and Trinidad and Tobago.

1960s: Experts studying the spread of the AIDS epidemic suggest that about 2,000 people in Africa may have been infected with HIV by the 1960s. Stored blood samples from a 1959 American malaria research project in the Congo proved one such example of early HIV infection.

1968: The Hong Kong Flu pandemic originated in China and lasted until 1969–70. It resulted in an estimated one million to four million deaths.

1968: A highly contagious pandemic, initiated by the emergence of a virus known as influenza A subtype H3N2, is suspected to have evolved from the strain of influenza that caused the pandemic of 1957.

Individuals who had been exposed to the 1957 virus apparently retained immune protection against the 1968 virus, explaining the mildness of the 1968 outbreak relative to the pandemic of 1918–19. The pandemic occurred in two waves, and, in most places, the second wave caused a greater number of deaths than the first wave.

1970s: HIV arrived in New York City precisely 10 years before doctors first noticed the disease. The virus passed from the Caribbean to New York in the early 1970s, where the disease gained a foothold for at least half a decade, before triggering outbreaks in places like San Francisco.

1970s: The first epidemic of HIV/AIDS is believed to have occurred in the Congolese capital, Kinshasa. The epidemic was accompanied by a surge in opportunistic infections, such as cryptococcal meningitis, Kaposi's sarcoma, tuberculosis, and specific forms of pneumonia.

1976: Three patients initiated a massive investigation from the CDC, which tracked the Legionnaires' disease outbreak (221 cases, including 34 deaths) to a bacterium in the hotel air conditioning system. The patients had all attended the same American Legion convention at Philadelphia's Bellevue-Stratford Hotel.

1976: Ebola, first discovered in bats, readily spreads to humans. Direct contact (through broken skin or mucous membranes) with an infected person or animal, or with objects such as contaminated needles and syringes, is the most common way the virus is spread. Symptoms may appear on average from eight to ten days after exposure and include fever, severe headache, muscle pain and weakness, diarrhea, vomiting, bleeding and bruising, and death.

1981: UCLA doctors reported the first cases of HIV/AIDS—initially described as an infectious cancer—among gay men living in Los Angeles. Because it takes 10 years, on average, for an infected person to show symptoms, these couldn't have been the first cases. Today, over 70 million people have been infected with HIV, and about 35 million have died from AIDS since the start of the pandemic.

1997: Approximately 1.5 million chickens and other poultry were slaughtered after the deadly bird flu, H5N1, infected and killed people.

2000: Measles, a highly contagious viral airborne disease, was declared eliminated in the U.S., meaning there was no continuous, endemic transmission. Prior to the 1963 vaccine, nearly every American teenager contracted measles by age 15, killing around 500 people each year.

2003: A federal judge ruled the Pentagon couldn't enforce mandatory anthrax vaccinations for military personnel.

2003: At the end of the year, severe acute respiratory syndrome (SARS) had killed 774 people out of a reported 8,098 infected. The main symptom was severe breathing difficulties, as almost all those infected developed pneumonia. SARS is caused by the previously unknown coronavirus, SARS-CoV-1, from the same family of viruses as COVID-19.

SARS started in Asia, and researchers have identified the most likely source as wild Chinese horseshoe bats that had been caught and brought to market. These bats harbored a SARS-like virus that subsequently infected civets before mutating, which meant that humans were now susceptible to the virus. Within a year, the infection had spread to more than two dozen countries.

2009: With swine flu reported in more than 70 nations, the World Health Organization declared the first global flu pandemic in 41 years. A(H1N1), the first major influenza outbreak of the 21st century, was unique for its rapid global spread and an unusually high degree of contagiousness. A series of reassortment events in pigs is believed to have caused the pandemic. WHO calculations and statistical models revealed that the total number of deaths may have been as high as 284,500 to 575,400.

2013: The western Africa nation Guinea reported an outbreak of the Ebola virus that lasted for two years.

2014 to 2016: The most significant outbreak of the Ebola virus in recorded history occurred in Guinea, Sierra Leone, and Liberia. Ebola is a hemorrhagic fever transmitted through direct contact with bodily fluids, with an average 50% fatality rate. It is caused by five different types of Ebola virus, four of which are known to inflict disease in humans. CDC reports indicated that 11,310 died during this recent outbreak.

2015–2016: Avian influenza outbreaks occurred among wild aquatic birds and spread to more susceptible farmed poultry. Millions of chickens, geese, and turkeys were destroyed to prevent further spread of the disease.

2016: The dangerous fungus known as Candida auris was first identified in the U.S. in 2016. The CDC has called Candida auris "an urgent antimicrobial resistance threat" because it is resistant to anti-fungal drugs and difficult to treat once an infection occurs. Candida auris mainly spreads in health care settings, where patients are sick and vulnerable.

2019: The Wuhan China health commission announced an outbreak of respiratory illness contracted at a seafood market in the city. The strain of viral pneumonia would eventually be known as COVID-19.

2019: SARS-CoV-2 (COVID-19), which experts thought was just another flu virus, began to create havoc around the world. The virus was noted for its rapid transmission and high fatality rates.

2020: In January, the U.S. reported its first known case after a Washington state resident returned from the coronavirus' Chinese epicenter. Chinese government experts confirmed human-to-human transmission of COVID-19—the worst worldwide catastrophe of the 21st century, with the highest death toll since the Spanish flu and World War II.

2020: After the WHO designated COVID-19 a pandemic, global stock markets and oil prices plunged, reflecting concern over the coronavirus. An alarmingly sharp slide at the opening bell on Wall Street triggered the first automatic halt in trading in more than two decades; the Dow industrials finished nearly 8% lower.

2020: The first COVID-19 vaccinations were implemented at U.S. nursing homes, where the virus killed 110,000 people. U.S. health officials warned that the coronavirus was certain to spread more widely in the U.S.; the CDC urged Americans to be prepared. 1.2 million deaths would be reported nationwide, even though President Trump affirmed the virus was "very well under control" in the United States.

2021: The Middle East Respiratory Syndrome (MERS) was a coronavirus infection with 886 associated deaths and a fatality rate of over 34%. Many cases were reported in Saudi Arabia and were linked to contact with camels or their dung, milk, or meat. MERS can cause severe respiratory and kidney failure.

2022: The Democratic Republic of Congo reported an outbreak of Mpox, an illness caused by the monkeypox virus, a species of the genus *Orthopoxvirus*. Common symptoms include a skin rash or mucosal lesions, which can last two to four weeks, accompanied by fever, headache, muscle aches, back pain, low energy, and swollen lymph nodes.

2022: More than 160 million chickens, ducks, turkeys, and other fowl were ordered euthanized after an H5N1 bird flu outbreak reached the United States in January and infected 67 people. Symptoms of human H5N1 infection may include pink eye, fever, fatigue, cough, muscle aches, sore throat, nausea and vomiting, diarrhea, stuffy or runny nose, and shortness of breath.

2023: Tuberculosis remains the top worldwide killer, caused by a bacterium called *Mycobacterium tuberculosis*. Over 50,000 people died from air-borne tuberculosis in Tanzania and Ethiopia alone, according to the World Health Organization. The highest number of tuberculosis cases in a decade killed 1.25 million people globally and infected 8 million. More than 9,600 cases were reported in the U.S.

2024: A more infectious version of mpox, first detected in the Democratic Republic of Congo, arrived in the U.S.—the first time the variant had spread outside Africa. Mpox is transmitted through close contact with someone with mpox, contaminated materials, or infected animals, and has largely impacted gay and bisexual men.

2024: A flu-like disease killed dozens of people in the Congo's Kwango province. Symptoms include fever, headache, cough, and anemia. Congo is already plagued by the mpox epidemic, with more than 47,000 suspected cases and more than 1,000 suspected deaths.

2024: To protect workers from the transmission of H5N1, federal health officials called for more testing of employees on farms with bird flu after a study showed some dairy workers had signs of infection, even when they didn't report feeling sick. Blood tests for farmworkers in Michigan and Colorado showed workers had antibodies indicative of contact with infected dairy cows or poultry.

2024: On October 30, 2024, the USDA reported an H5N1 infection in a pig—the first report of its kind in the U.S. According to the CDC:

> *The discovery that an avian influenza A virus has infected a new mammal species is always concerning, especially when the virus is detected in pigs, which are susceptible to influenza viruses circulating in pigs, humans, birds, and other species. These viruses can swap genes through a process called genetic reassortment, which can occur when two (or more) influenza viruses infect a single host.*

Reassortment can result in the emergence of new influenza A viruses with new or different properties, such as the ability to spread more easily among animals or people.

2024: As of November 10, 2024, researchers have confirmed 7,073,453 COVID-induced deaths worldwide, with an estimated 19.1 to 36 million COVID-induced "excess deaths."

2024: The Agriculture Department ordered testing of the nation's milk supply for bird flu. Testing began in six states—California, Colorado, Michigan, Mississippi, Oregon, and Pennsylvania, aimed at eliminating the virus, which has infected more than 700 dairy herds in 15 states.

2024–2025: In late January 2025, the weekly rate of flu hospitalizations reached the highest level observed during all flu seasons since 2010. The 2024–2025 flu season has caused an estimated 24 million cases, 310,000 hospitalizations, and 15,000 deaths so far, the CDC says. The death toll could reach up to 65,000 by the end of the season, per preliminary estimates from the CDC.

2025: The World Organization for Animal Health reported the first confirmed case of H5N9 (a less researched subtype of bird flu), detected on a California duck farm. The Highly Pathogenic Avian Influenza (HPAI) appeared in China more than a decade ago and is thought to come from a genetic combination of other bird flu viruses, including H5N1.

2025: The Department of Agriculture reported that a case of HPAI struck a poultry producer in Georgia, the nation's top state for chicken production. It was the first outbreak since 2022.

2025: On January 06, 2025, the Louisiana Department of Health reported the first human death from H5N1. The patient, over age 65, reportedly had underlying medical conditions and represents Louisiana's only human case of H5N1 and the nation's first severe case of a mutated bird flu virus.

2025: One sample from a remote part of northern Tanzania tested positive for Marburg disease, a highly infectious virus which is fatal in up to 88% of cases, alarmingly, with no authorized vaccine or treatment. Like Ebola, the Marburg virus originates in fruit bats and spreads between people through close contact with the bodily fluids of infected individuals.

2025: U.S. regulators banned the dye called Red 3 from the nation's food supply, nearly 35 years after it was barred from cosmetics because of potential cancer risk. The dye is known as erythrosine, FD&C Red No. 3, or Red 3. The ban removes it from the list of approved color additives in foods, dietary supplements, and oral medicines, such as cough syrups.

2025: A new COVID-19 Nimbus variant is causing "razor blade" sore throats and driving a rise in COVID cases globally. By mid-May, the new variant had reached nearly 11% of sequenced samples reported globally.

10

THE DOOMSDAY FISH

"Here Be Monsters" is a warning often inscribed on the maps and charts of ancient mariners who feared that sea serpents, like the Kraken, lurked in the ocean's depths. A gigantic sea serpent consuming an entire ship, including the crew, can be seen in 16th-century engravings. Cryptozoologists have suggested that relic marine reptiles, such as *Architeuthis*, a species of giant squid, or the cryptic Doomsday Fish, may be responsible for such reports.

Described as a "sea serpent," the Doomsday Fish is an elusive species, believed to be an omen of impending disaster. Scientifically known as the oarfish (*Regalecus glesne*), the ribbon-like silvery organism lives as much as 3,000 feet below the ocean's surface, dwelling on the edge of the mesopelagic zone, the sea's least explored ecosystem. Known as the "Twilight Zone," the Mesopelagic Zone extends from 3,300 feet below the surface of the ocean, to the epipelagic zone. It sits between the epipelagic zone, which receives the most light, and the bathy-pelagic zone, which receives no light. It is a deep-sea dweller, evolved to withstand the immense pressure of its environment. This unique adaptation, however, makes it unable to survive in shallow depths, which is why it is rarely observed alive.

The oarfish are considered the longest bony fish in the world, with lengths estimated at over 30 feet. In the 1960s, scientists spotted an oarfish estimated to be about 50 feet long, while unverified sightings claim specimens of more than 100 feet long. These are mysterious creatures. Marine biologists are curious about the evolutionary adaptations that enable them to thrive in deep-sea environments, and there is little known about oarfish biology, anatomy, and life history.

The deep-water creature was spotted off the shores of Encinitas, California, in November 2024. What was alarming was that only 22 oarfish sightings had been observed over the past century, until three were seen within three months—a rare occurrence. Another alarm that has been sounding is the San Andreas Fault, a significant gash in the Earth's crust, located in western North America. The fault has been associated with tectonic movements that caused earthquakes in 1906, 1989, and 1994, and, according to the doomsayers, will inevitably cause California to sink into the sea. The majority of California's population lives in its vicinity. In 1906, the deadliest earthquake in U.S. history struck San Francisco, killing more than 3,000 people, and was followed by raging fires across the city. The earthquake was estimated to have reached as high as 8.3 on the Richter scale, and experts have predicted there will be more.

Days before a 6.7-magnitude earthquake struck the southern part of the Philippines in 2017, oarfish, some dead and some near dying, washed ashore. Oceanologists theorized that the tectonic movements preceding earthquakes kill the fish, causing them to wash up on beaches. Others believe there is something more ominous in play.

In March 2011, months before the country's largest recorded earthquake, at least a dozen oarfish were reported on Japan's coastline, according to the Ocean Conservancy. The Tohoku earthquake and resulting tsunami killed nearly 20,000 people and triggered the infamous nuclear accident at the Fukushima power plant. The Fukushima disaster was not unexpected, because Japanese mythology foretells that sightings of doomsday fish are precursors to earthquakes and tsunamis.

Doomsday fish have been described in ancient Japanese folklore. Ryugu no Tsukai was believed to have a snakelike body with a woman's head. It was the messenger of an aquatic deity and associated with Jinja Hime, another servant of the sea god. According to legend, both creatures possessed the supernatural ability to predict natural disasters. Writing for *Discovery Magazine*, Stephen C. George stated:

> *For hundreds of years, mariners and fishermen knew this sea creature as a herald of woe. Seeing one in the water or even washed up on shore was an omen, a warning of some impending disaster, typically a natural one, such as an earthquake or tsunami. In Japan, the creature was named "ryugu no tsukai," a messenger from the palace of the sea god. Others dramatically dubbed it the Harbinger of Doom, or simply the Doomsday Fish.*

The Ten-Year Apocalypse

Omens of the end times have appeared in ancient and modern times. One of history's cruelest natural disasters was an apocalyptic event in the "Dirty Thirties." Many God-fearing pioneers believed the Dust Bowl was connected to ancient biblical prophecies and that they were living in the end times. There were reasons for this rationale. Randall J. Stephens wrote that during the Dust Bowl, religious fundamentalism—described as being "typically white, southern, and militant" —was based on key fundamentals:

> *Usually included a firm stance on the infallibility of the Bible, the Virgin birth of Jesus, the reality of sin, the need for salvation, the resurrection of Jesus, the validity of miracles, and the significance of prophecy and signs of the end of the world.*

They were known as dirt storms, sandstorms, black blizzards, and "dusters," but the devastating "Black Sunday" that blasted across the High Plains on April 14, 1935, was a mountain of swirling doom that transformed a warm, sunny afternoon into a nightmare. Black Sunday was only one part of the Ten-Year Apocalypse, an ecological monster that was part Kraken and part seven-headed cobra.

Within a relatively short span of time, the Dust Bowl created enormous socioeconomic upheaval, and the largest migration in American history. Three and a half million people abandoned their wind-blasted farms. Some in Oklahoma, Arkansas, Missouri, Iowa, Nebraska, Kansas, Texas, Colorado, and New Mexico said they were cursed and headed west to California's Promised Land. Others took to the road as marauding tramps, joining hobo camps and communes for survival. After the dust from the Great Plains traveled all the way to the East Coast, blotting out the sun over the nation's capital, the Soil Conservation Act was passed. But it was a little too late, and the damage had been done. America's breadbasket was ruined.

Measured in black blizzards and mouthfuls of misery, the possibility of the end times was evident. But how could anyone survive? And what could Christian preachers say to inspire the downtrodden with sermons about a loving and merciful God?

Fundamentalists believe in New Testament prophecies and warnings about the world's end. Firm in biblical teachings, they oppose liberalism in churches and secularism in society. Many looked back at the time of the Mormon Armageddon, when founder Joseph Smith called a meeting of his church leaders (1835) to announce that God had spoken to him. Smith revealed that Jesus would return within the next 56 years, after which, the end times would begin. Mormons believe that during the "latter days," there will be a period of destruction and the Second Coming of Christ, when a new Jerusalem will restore Earth to a state of righteousness. Susan Donaldson James' article *Apocalypse Now: Floods, Tornadoes, Locusts: Is violent weather around the globe a sign of a coming Apocalypse?* observed that:

*God's wrath seems at work these days, as the heavens and Earth
have unleashed earthquakes in China, a cyclone in Burma, killer
tornadoes and record floods across the U.S. and even a plague of
locusts (cicadas) in New England. Though tsunamis, hurricanes
and heat waves may not be a punishment from God, history
teaches that events in the physical world trigger upheaval in society. Civilizations have risen and fallen over drought, famine, and
water wars.*

The Locust Plague

Midwestern farmers suffered soaring temperatures, hail, and barb-
wire winds for the good part of a decade. Local fairs were canceled
because no one had any produce. It was all too clear. Because of their
sins, a plague straight out of the Old Testament was to be their
punishment. All hope for normalcy ended. Messy Nessy wrote that
residents of the Great Plains believed the Dust Bowl signaled the end
of the world:

*For nearly a decade, relentless dust storms of biblical proportions
rolled in like moving mountains 200 miles wide... Likened to the
stories out of the Old Testament in Egypt, the dust storms didn't just
kill the cattle and annihilate crops, they brought about plagues of
locusts and herds of hungry Jack rabbits scouring the land for food
because nature had become so unbalanced.*

It was a scourge of biblical proportions, and yes, we had already been
warned that it was coming. The Book of Revelation forewarned of
pain and suffering during the end times and the torment of scorpions
and locusts:

*In those days, men "would seek death but not find it and shall desire
to die, but death will flee from them. And the locusts would not kill
them, but that they should be tormented five months: and their
torment was as the torment of a scorpion when he striketh a man.*

Described as "evil forces," locusts are mentioned in the Bible over 30 times. Detailed images of crop devastation are found in Exodus, Psalms, Jeremiah, Joel, and Revelation. One memorable mention is a terrifying metaphor found in Revelation 9:2-10 (KJV), in which a menacing army is described as a vast cloud of locusts swarming out of a bottomless pit:

> And the shapes of the locusts were like unto horses prepared unto battle, and on their heads were crowns like gold, and their faces were like the faces of men. And they had hair as the hair of women, and their teeth were as the teeth of lions. And they had breastplates, as it were breastplates of iron; and the sound of their wings was as the sound of chariots of many horses running to battle. And they had tails like unto scorpions, and there were stings in their tails: and their power was to hurt men five months.

Attempts to eradicate the insects were futile. Farmers attempted all sorts of remedies, including the 80,000 pounds of bran and 400 pounds of sodium arsenate distributed by the county agricultural agent. But nothing worked. The grasshoppers stayed and laid eggs. The Adams County Nebraska Historical Society described hordes of locusts being so dense they clogged a mighty combine, causing it to break down:

> The next curse to fall upon the Plainsmen was grasshoppers, plagues of them reminding the faithful of biblical scriptures. Although some grasshoppers had showed up in 1935, they appeared in force in Adams County in 1936, with especially heavy flights on June 24, and July 1. The insects ate vegetable gardens, covered the air with the sight and sound of their activity. Farther south, into Kansas, the grasshoppers stripped foliage from evergreen trees, gnawed bark from young trees.

An alarming fact about locusts is that a 10- to 16-fold increase in numbers occurs from generation to generation. According to religious writer Betty Dunn:

African countries are now experiencing their worst infestations of locusts in decades. Desert locusts in Africa and Asia swarm with as many as 150 million locusts per square kilometer and fly in the direction of the prevailing wind. They may travel up to 150 kilometers in one day. A tiny, one-kilometer locust swarm can eat the same amount of food in a day as about 35,000 people.

But, as science monitored the Dust Bowl's madness, the literary community turned the aching heartbreak of the "Dirty Thirties" into the poetry of Apocalyptic Awe. Singer-songwriter Woody Guthrie composed *Dusty Old Dust* (1940) about the apocalyptical event; it became known as the foreboding *So Long, It's Been Good to Know Yuh*:

So long, it's been good to know yuh;
So long, it's been good to know yuh;
So long, it's been good to know yuh.
This dusty old dust is a-gettin' my home,
And I got to be driftin' along.

Director Christopher Nolan's science fiction epic *Interstellar* (2014), set in the year 2067, consisted of interviews with survivors of an apocalyptic dust bowl. Although Nolan's film is fictional, he used real interview clips of survivors of the Dust Bowl. John Steinbeck's *The Grapes of Wrath* (1939) looked at how the Dust Bowl brought humankind to the brink. Called "the conscience of America," Steinbeck (1902–1968) was awarded the Pulitzer Prize in 1940, but the Associated Farmers saw Steinbeck's novel through a different lens and criticized the book's perceived "socialistic" tone:

The only inference that can be obtained from Steinbeck's book is that he is proposing exactly the same sort of overthrow of the present form of government and the substitution of collective agriculture as did Carey McWilliams in his Factories in the Fields.

The Associated Farmers said that "we would not want our women and children to read so vulgar a book." Steinbeck's "vulgar" book, which described the American spirit of working together to survive, won the Nobel Prize for Literature in 1962.

The Year 2024

If American pioneers were able to uncover omens warning of the impending Dust Bowl, then modern-day pioneers should have plenty of omens to choose from. Researchers claim that the planet is getting hotter and our weather patterns more extreme, as fossil fuel emissions heat the atmosphere in "climate breakdown." New data from the European Copernicus climate service says 2024 was the world's hottest on record, with the last 10 years the warmest. World Weather Attribution (WWA) and Climate Central scientists found that in 2024, we suffered an average of 41 extra days of dangerous heat because of human-caused climate change. Global heat records made 2024 likely the hottest year ever measured. Friederike Otto, the lead WWA climate scientist, issued a dire analysis:

> *The finding is devastating but utterly unsurprising: Climate change played a role, and often a major role, in most of the events we studied. It made heat, droughts, tropical cyclones, and heavy rainfall more likely and more intense worldwide, destroying the lives and livelihoods of millions and often uncounted numbers of people.*

Otto cautioned, "As long as the world keeps burning fossil fuels, this will only get worse." Climate change and El Niño weather patterns played a role in creating warmer ocean waters that fueled more destructive storms. In the French archipelago of Mayotte, a hundred-year category-4 storm, Cyclone Chido, with winds above 136 miles per hour, ripped across the Indian Ocean nation in 2024. It was the strongest storm to hit the islands in more than 90 years, inflicting devastation "likened to an atomic bomb," with hundreds of feared victims.

Most Polluting

According to Climate Trace, an organization co-founded by former U.S. Vice President Al Gore, cities in Asia and the United States emit the most heat-trapping greenhouse gasses that feed climate change, with Shanghai the most polluting. Others in the top 40 include Tokyo (#2—250 million metric tons), New York City (#3—160 million metric tons), Houston (#4—150 million metric tons), and Seoul, South Korea (#5—142 million metric tons).

The 2024 report also examined traditional pollutants such as carbon monoxide, volatile organic compounds, ammonia, sulfur dioxide, and other chemicals associated with dirty air. Earth's total carbon dioxide and methane pollution grew 0.7% to 61.2 billion metric tons, with short-lived but extra-potent methane rising 0.2%. During that same month, authorities in New Delhi, India, shut schools, halted construction, and banned non-essential trucks from entering the city after air pollution shot up to its worst level during that year.In several city areas, pollution levels were more than 50 times higher than the WHO's recommended safe limit.

In 2015, nearly 200 nations meeting in Paris adopted the first global pact to fight climate change, calling it "a significant step towards a more sustainable future." The world was asked to collectively cut greenhouse gas emissions and limit global warming to 2.7 degrees Fahrenheit. Although these proposals hold the promise of a healthier planet, the reality suggests something else. Numerous critics have charged that calls to reduce pollution are often seen as splendid examples of "empty climate pageantry" and opportunities to make "sanctimonious speeches" on large global stages. The estimated cost of replacing fossil fuels with green energies is $27 trillion annually across the century, making it unattainable for poorer, undeveloped nations who are in the eye of the raging storm that has already been visited upon us—as evidenced in the following chapter.

11

NATURAL DISASTERS

Dystopian weather events are getting stronger and more frequent. Because of global warming, hurricanes, tornados, floods, and fires are increasing and worsening. Adding to the dread are slick, well-spoken meteorologists with a bizarre doomsday vocabulary—*firenado, snowmageddon, thundersnow, bomb cyclone, derecho,* and even *gully washer, mackerel sky, and dust devils.*

This is the six o'clock onslaught of doom, warning that so-called "hundred-year events" are inevitable. Hundred-year storms are statistical tools used by meteorologists and climatologists to determine the likelihood of intense storms or floods, typically misinterpreted by the public. Writer Rick Rycroft attempted to clear up the common misunderstanding that such storms come only once a century:

> *For meteorologists, the one in-100-year event is an event of a size that will be equaled or exceeded on average once every 100 years. This means that over 1,000 years, you would expect the one in the 100-year event to be equaled or exceeded ten times. However, several of those ten times might happen within a few years of each other, and then there might be none for a long time afterward.*

Two statistics help clarify these events: (1) There is approximately a 63.4% chance of a 100-year flood occurring in any 100 years. (2) In any given year, there is a 1% chance of an event of at least that size, known as an "annual exceedance probability." Past catastrophic events, spanning over 100 years of storm warnings and mandatory evacuations, are listed here. We can argue the cause, but we cannot argue their deadly consequences or predict when the next will be unleashed.

1755: Called "the most notable earthquake of history" by Nelson's Encyclopedia, the Great Lisbon earthquake took place on November 1, 1755, destroying that great city in less than 10 minutes.

1839: The Coringa cyclone. India's Coringa Cyclone was the first weather event in human history known as a cyclone, a word coined by Henry Piddington, an official of the British East India Company, meaning "the coil of a snake." Death toll: 300,000.

1883: The Krakatoa volcanic eruption. VEI 6. (The volcanic explosivity index (VEI) is a scale used to measure the size of explosive volcanic eruptions). The April 26, 1883, explosions destroyed the entire Krakatoa Island and created a tsunami with waves up to 140 feet. The final blast was the loudest recorded sound in history, heard on 10% of Earth's surface, according NOAA. Death toll: 36,000.

1889: The Johnstown flood. After several days of drenching rain, a dam on Pennsylvania's Lake Conemaugh washed away. The collapse unleashed some 16 million tons of water, which quickly turned into a 40-foot-high, half mile-wide surge of mud and debris. An hour later, the wave struck Johnstown, crushing some 1,600 buildings and sweeping away everything in its path. Death toll: over 2,200.

1895: A tsunami triggered by a magnitude 8.5 earthquake struck the coast of northeastern Japan with waves reaching 125 feet high. Death toll: more than 22,000.

1896: The Great St. Louis tornado. EF4. (The Enhanced Fujita Scale measures the intensity of tornadoes). On May 27, 1896, the Great St. Louis tornado wreaked havoc across St. Louis, Missouri and East St.

Louis, Illinois, with winds of 168 to 199 mph. In addition to destroying countless structures, the tornado also tore away 300 feet of the Eads Bridge, the first bridge to be constructed of true steel, and touted as tornado-proof. Death toll: at least 255, and more than 1,000 injured.

1900: The Galveston hurricane. Category 4. The powerful hurricane remains the deadliest natural disaster in U.S. history, causing widespread destruction and flooding. In response to the devastation, Galveston built a protective seawall and elevated parts of the city to reduce the risk of future storms. Death toll: 8,000 to 12,000.

1902: The Santa María eruption. VEI 6. Guatemala's Santa Maria event was one of the biggest volcanic explosions of the 20th century, leaving a crater nearly a mile across.

1906: The San Francisco earthquake. 7.9 magnitude. The quake was followed by a massive fire that swept from the business section and continued for four days, until its smoldering ashes were extinguished by rain. In the process, more than 500 blocks in the city center— covering some 4 square miles—were leveled. Death toll: as many as 3,000. Estimated damage: $350 million. Some 28,000 buildings were destroyed.

1908: A major earthquake followed by a tsunami devastated the Italian cities of Messina and Reggio Calabria. Death toll: at least 70,000.

May 18, 1910: Halley's Comet passed by Earth, brushing it with its tail.

1910: The Great Fire of 1910, also known as the Big Burn or Big Blow Up, was the largest wildfire in American history, burning more than 3 million acres of drought-stricken forest across Montana, Idaho, and Washington, as wildfires were whipped into tornado-like flamethrowers by 70-mph winds. Thousands of soldiers and fire-fighters were deployed. Death toll: 87, including 78 firefighters.

1925: The Tri-State tornado. F5. On March 18, 1925, "the deadliest tornado in U.S. history" tore a 219-mile-long path across Missouri,

Illinois, and Indiana. It was the longest path of a tornado in recorded history, estimated to be about a mile wide and with winds over 300 mph. The tornado destroyed more than 19 communities, including over 15,000 homes. Death toll: unknown.

1928: The St. Francis Dam north of Los Angeles, California failed, sending over 12 billion gallons of water into San Francisquito Canyon. Death toll: more than 400.

1930–1936: The Dust Bowl was no natural disaster but the greatest man-made environmental catastrophe in American history. (1) Millions of acres were plowed in order to grow wheat. (2) Years of overcultivation and poor land management ensued. (3) Severe droughts, lasting for years, persisted in a region that typically received less than 20 inches of annual rainfall. (4). The exposed topsoil, robbed of native grasses and water-retaining roots, was blown away by heavy spring winds. (5) An estimated 1.1 billion metric tons of soil were lost across about 156,000 square miles of the Great Plains between 1934 and 1935, the drought's most severe period. (6) The Soil Conservation Act was passed before the end of 1935, after dust from the Great Plains blew all the way to the East Coast, blotting out the sun over the nation's capital.

1931: The Central China flood. Heavy snowmelt, torrential rains, and seven different cyclonic storms combined to produce the most devastating flood in Chinese history. The Yangtze, Yellow, and Huai Rivers burst through their poorly managed dikes and flooded an area larger than England. Death toll: as many as 3.7 million died from drowning, widespread famine, and outbreaks of cholera, typhoid fever, and dysentery.

1935: They were known as dirt storms, sandstorms, black blizzards, and "dusters," but the devastating Black Sunday that blasted the High Plains was attributed to dry weather and years of poor soil conservation. On April 14, 1935, a mountain of blackness swept across the High Plains and transformed a warm, sunny afternoon into a horrible blackness.

1946: A magnitude 8.6 earthquake centered near Alaska's Aleutian Islands triggered a tsunami that pounded the Hawaiian Islands with waves up to 55 feet tall. Death toll: 159.

1953: One of the deadliest tornadoes in Texas history devastated the city of Waco. Death toll: 114, and nearly 600 injured.

1964: Alaska was hit by a magnitude 9.2 earthquake (still the strongest on record in North America) and tsunamis. Death toll: more than 130.

1972: Hurricane Agnes. Category 1. At the time, Agnes was the costliest hurricane to ever have hit the United States, with much of the affected in the northeastern United States. The widespread flooding from this storm caused Agnes to be called the most destructive hurricane in United States history, impacting 12 states. Flood damage was heaviest in Pennsylvania, where Agnes was the state's wettest tropical cyclone. Due to the significant effects, the name Agnes was retired in the spring of 1973. Death toll: 128.

1977: In aviation's deadliest disaster, a KLM Boeing 747, attempting to take off in heavy fog, crashed into a Pan Am 747 on an airport runway on the Canary Island of Tenerife. Death toll: 583.

1988: Armenia earthquake. A major earthquake in the Soviet Union devastated northern Armenia. Death toll: at least 25,000.

1991: Mount Pinatubo in the northern Philippines erupted. Death toll: more than 800.

1992: Hurricane Andrew. Category 5. Andrew leveled entire neighborhoods with 175 mph winds, displacing tens of thousands of residents in South Florida. Andrew's impact led to a complete overhaul of Florida's building codes and changes in hurricane preparedness practices nationwide. Death toll: 65. Estimated damage: over $27 billion; one of the costliest natural disasters in U.S. history.

1994: The Northridge earthquake rattled the Los Angeles area. The magnitude 6.7 quake caused an estimated $25 billion in damages. Death toll: 57, and 9,000 injuries.

1995: An earthquake with a magnitude of 7.2 struck the city of Kobe, Japan. Death toll: more than 6,000.

1999: The Bridge Creek–Moore tornado struck the Oklahoma City metropolitan area, causing 41 deaths and nearly 600 injuries; the tornado's top wind speed of 321 miles per hour was the highest ever recorded on Earth.

2004: The Indian Ocean tsunami and 9.1-magnitude earthquake. On the day after Christmas, 2004, a catastrophic earthquake struck undersea off the west coast of Sumatra, Indonesia. The tsunami wave reached over 100 feet high, traveling as fast as 500 mph. This event is considered the third largest earthquake in the world since 1900. Death toll: 230,000—more than any other tsunami in recorded history. More than 170,000 died in Indonesia alone. It displaced nearly 2 million people in 14 South Asian and East African countries. Estimated damage: $10 billion.

2005: Hurricane Katrina. Category 5. Katrina made landfall as a weakened Category 3 hurricane, primarily affecting New Orleans and the Gulf Coast. Catastrophic flooding left nearly 80% of the city underwater after the levees in New Orleans failed. Estimated damage: $125 billion. Death toll: over 1,800.

2008: A devastating 7.9 magnitude earthquake in China's Sichuan province was among the worst in the country's history. Death toll: more than 7,000 dead or missing.

2010: The Haiti earthquake. 7.0. The epicenter of the earthquake was approximately 16 miles west of the capital Port-au-Prince. It caused severe damage to buildings, infrastructure, and other critical facilities, including 1.5 million homes. Death toll: 200,000.

2011: Joplin, Missouri tornado. EF5. "The deadliest tornado in modern U.S. history," with a path length of 22 miles and up to a mile wide at its maximum point, struck Joplin on May 22, 2011. Estimated damage: $2.8 billion. Death toll: 160, and nearly 1,000 injured.

2011: The Great East Japan earthquake. Considered the fourth most powerful earthquake since modern seismography began in 1900 and Japan's largest ever recorded earthquake, the event triggered powerful tsunami waves (up to 133 feet high and 435 mph) and a nuclear accident at the Fukushima Daiichi power plant. Estimated damage: $34.6 billion. Death toll: nearly 20,000.

2018: Hurricane Michael. Category 5. Michael made landfall in the Florida Panhandle as one of the strongest storms to hit the continental U.S. Michael's winds and storm surge caused widespread destruction, particularly in Mexico Beach and Panama City. Estimated damage: $25 billion. Death toll: 59.

2019: Venice saw its worst flooding in more than 50 years, with the water reaching 6.14 feet above average sea level. Estimated damage: Hundreds of millions of dollars.

2019: Tropical cyclones Idai and Kenneth. In what was called the worst natural disaster to hit southern Africa in at least two decades, two cyclones pummeled Mozambique over a period of two months. On March 4, Idai made landfall at the port of Beira, and six weeks later, Kenneth made landfall in northern Mozambique—the first time two strong tropical cyclones have hit the country in the same season. Death toll: 603.

2022: The Tonga Volcano. VEI 5.7 The eruption released 50 million tons of water vapor into the atmosphere, equivalent to more than 100 Hiroshima bombs and enough to warm the planet for years. The Kingdom of Tonga blast extended for 162 miles with a pillar of ash, steam, and gas that stretched 12 miles into the air, the tallest in recorded history, according to the National Oceanic and Atmospheric Administration (NOAA).

2024: Hurricane Helene. Category 5. On September 26, Helene struck Florida's Big Bend with 140-mph winds and a 15-foot storm surge, devastating parts of the southeastern United States and dumping over 30 inches of rain in parts of North Carolina. Helene was the deadliest hurricane in the United States since 2005's Katrina. It was also the seventh most expensive storm in American history. Estimated damage: $124 billion. Death toll: at least 249.

2025: Los Angeles has been overwhelmed with destructive wildfires fueled by high-wind cyclones and a lack of rain.

2025: The climate monitoring group, Berkeley Earth, warned that "Things aren't just getting worse. They're getting worse faster." By 2028, so much greenhouse gasses will have been released that a key threshold for limiting global warming will have been passed, spawning more frequent and severe climate extremes—unprecedented heat waves, droughts, extreme rainfall events, and bigger storms.

12

THE MOTHMAN PROPHECIES

Historians cite the Silver Bridge collapse as one of the worst bridge disasters in U.S. history. The structure connected Point Pleasant, West Virginia with Gallipolis, Ohio. When it opened, it was the nation's first bridge to use an innovative eyebar-link suspension system, rather than traditional wire-cable suspension. But after paranormal researchers began to investigate and talk to witnesses, Silver Bridge took on a more sinister aura.

December 15, 1967, was a special day. It was rush hour, the bridge bumper-to-bumper, about a week before Christmas. And then the nightmare. On that fateful day, 31 vehicles plunged into the icy waters of the Ohio River, claiming 46 lives from drowning and from being crushed by chunks of the bridge landing on top of their vehicles.

First opened in 1928, the Silver Bridge had been designed by the JE Greiner Company and built by the precursor to the West Virginia-Ohio Bridge Company and American Bridge Company. It took a year to complete the two-lane, 1,760-foot eyebar-suspension bridge, but, according to writer Marco Margaritoff, from the very beginning, the builders cut corners:

The bridge was originally meant to be suspended with traditional wire cables. However, an alternate bid for an eyebar design ended up being cheaper. Plus, this design would make the bridge one of the first structures of its kind in the United States.

Silver Bridge: Believed to be the worst bridge disaster in U.S. history, the structure had connected Point Pleasant, West Virginia with Gallipolis, Ohio.

But decades later, its design failed to meet modern standards. When the Silver Bridge was first built, in the 1920s, the average car weighed about 1,500 pounds. By the 1960s, most cars weighed about 3,000 pounds, and almost 4,000 of these heavier vehicles crossed the bridge daily, causing unanticipated stress on the eyebars.

The disaster immediately evoked the 1940 collapse of the Tacoma Narrows Bridge, the world's third-longest suspension bridge, which collapsed only four months after it opened. Arch 20, a website promoting professional collaboration in architecture, noted the shared cost-cutting measures of the two bridge builds:

In an attempt to try to keep costs down, cheap girders were chosen, causing the bridge to buckle and sway along its suspended length - under regular wind forces! Due to the torsional motion, the bridge was subject to, the towers holding the spans were pulled inward, cracks formed, and finally, the entire bridge crashed into the river.

John A. Keel

History has determined that Silver Bridge was a failure of engineering technology and oversight, contradicting any bizarre association to Mothman. That association inspired several important books, including Gray Barker's *Silver Bridge* (1970), John Keel's *The Mothman Prophesies* (1975), and a motion picture of the same name. *Mothman* checked all the boxes; it was interesting, controversial, and marketable. Keel and Barker articulated the disaster's paranormal elements, suggesting a juncture where science and the supernatural collided with reality. This story would grow larger in its retellings.

John A. Keel (1930–2009), American journalist, UFO specialist, monster hunter, and self-described demonologist, was a unique contributor to the paranormal genre. He witnessed his first UFO in space 1954, while on a trip to Egypt; he described a circular spinning object hovering in the sky above the Aswan Dam in broad daylight:

> *The thing I saw was Saturn-shaped and it appeared the center was not moving but the outside was spinning... it was a very odd thing, and various people were looking at it with me.*

Keel, who was a remarkable example of Indiana Jones' bravado, spent three years travelling through the Middle East and Asia and glimpsed a yeti while crossing into the Himalayan state of Sikkim. At 27, Keel wrote his autobiography, *Jadoo: Mysteries of the Orient* (1957.)

Years later, Keel's book, *The Mothman Prophesies*, investigated sightings of a creature called Mothman, who, during 1966 and 1967, terrorized Point Pleasant, West Virginia, in the heart of an abandoned munitions site. Described as a large, winged humanoid with glowing red eyes, its most famous sighting was on November 15, 1966. Sightings continued for 13 months until the bridge disaster.

The Mothman Prophesies describes alleged sightings (numerous and credible) of the winged creature and also UFO theories and supernatural phenomena related to the bridge collapse. After sightings of the Mothman began in 1966, the town was plunged into a state of terror. People reported seeing the creature everywhere—in the woods, on the roads, and even perched on their rooftops. But was this a creature from another dimension, a harbinger of doom, or a mass hallucination?

Director Mark Pellington adapted Keel's book to the screen and claimed *The Mothman Prophecies* (2002) was "based on true events." Pellington depicted the creature as an ancient, unknowable supernatural omen and not as a monster or cryptid, interpreting Keel's storyline as "a psychological mystery with surreal overtones." Pellington asked the apocalyptic question, "What happens when sane, reasonable people are faced with the unbelievable... in this case, a harbinger of death?"

Some people, like G.D. Pickering, author of *Mysterious Creatures: The Mothman of Point Pleasant* (2023), repeated that question, inferring that Mothman was a messenger from beyond warning us of impending doom.

Still, the explanations were as interesting as the topic of discussion. A *Soldier of Fortune* magazine article titled *UFO Mystery Solved: "Mothmen" Were Actually Green Berets* (2014) was written by Harold Hutchison, who claimed the Mothman scare was created by Green Berets, and that during the 1960s, the Defense Logistics Agency maintained a facility in the Ohio Valley area and covertly tested "the high-altitude, low-opening (HALO) freefall parachuting technique," using luminous paint, to be utilized later in Vietnam. But William Grabowski has an opinion on that:

> *So, the* Soldier of Fortune *article is itself a curious (and poorly edited) mystery. Is it yet another example of disinformation*

designed to keep us away from "the truth"? If so, why? After so long,
who, in Intelligence circles, really cares?

Who knows? Theories range from aspects of the paranormal to misidentifications, inspiring books, a film, and a yearly festival in Point Pleasant. In 2003, at the second annual Mothman Festival, Keel unveiled a 12-foot-tall metal sculpture of the Mothman by artist Bob Roach, based on a Frank Fazetta painting.

National Transportation Safety Board

It wasn't until April 1971 when the National Transportation Safety Board officially determined the bridge collapse was caused by stress corrosion cracking in a suspension chain's eyebar:

A cleavage fracture in the lower limb of the eye of eyebar 330... The
fracture was caused by the development of a critical-size flaw over
the 40-year life of the structure as the result of the joint action of
stress corrosion and corrosion fatigue.

Though these eyebars were vital for the structural integrity of the bridge, there was no way to properly inspect them without taking them apart. Still, the Silver Bridge was regularly inspected, and, after one 1965 inspection, underwent about $30,000 in repairs. Two further inspections followed in the summer of 1967, but inspectors were unable to detect problems with the bridge's eyebars, as documented by West Virginia's Public Broadcasting:

One of those eyebars had a small, unseen defect. The faulty eyebar
eventually cracked and began to corrode, out of sight from the
public or bridge inspectors. At about 5 p.m. on December 15, the
eyebar failed, setting off a series of other failures that caused the
bridge to collapse.

As we experience apocalyptical anxiety, there remains little doubt that many of humankind's most devastating events are more mundane. They are not due to political, religious, or meteorological admonitions, but to human error. As an example, the Silver Bridge catastrophe was a quagmire of faulty eyebar construction, an overload of traffic, and insufficient inspection.

Silver Bridge led to national changes in how bridges were inspected. A year later, it was replaced by the Silver Memorial Bridge, about a mile south of the old structure. And at St. Mary's—some 100 miles upstream from Point Pleasant—another 40-year-old bridge of the same design was immediately closed and demolished.

The following chapter is a listing of man-made disasters that, like a row of falling dominoes, seems never-ending. The list of catastrophes is constant and, as some believe, almost predictable, intermingling with the strange bedfellows of science and the paranormal.

13

MAN-MADE DISASTERS

Man-made catastrophes, including pollution, nuclear meltdowns, mining disasters, chemical explosions, and underwater oil spills, are the pound of flesh traded for progress. Technological disasters caused by human error, careless safety protocols, neglected building regulations, and man-made climate change, which instigates higher temperatures and extreme weather patterns, are the price we pay for fusing nature and technology and inviting inevitable disaster. The following is a list of disasters befalling those who carve tunnels into the ground, build bridges across rivers, and climb skyscrapers rising into the skies.

1871: The Great Chicago Fire burned for more than 24 hours, sweeping through the heart of Chicago, killing 300 people and leaving one-third of the city's population homeless. The tragic legend of "Mrs. O'Leary's cow" remains the most well-known of theories about how Chicago's Great Fire started, but *Smithsonian* observed:

> *While there is little doubt that the fire started in a barn owned by Patrick and Catherine O'Leary, the exact cause of the fire remains a*

mystery. From the barn at 137 DeKoven Street, on the city's south-
west side, the fire spread north and east, into the heart of Chicago's
business district.

The fire burned an area four miles long and one mile wide, destroying 17,500 buildings and 73 miles of street. One theory proposed that a thief knocked over a kerosene lantern while stealing milk from O'Leary's barn, and, years later, Louis M. Cohn confessed to starting the fire by knocking over a lantern when running away from an illegal card game. But brokenhearted Catherine O'Leary was the real victim. Newspapers called her "shiftless and worthless" and a "drunken old hag with dirty hands." P.T. Barnum invited her to tour with his circus. Robert McNamera wrote:

Mrs. O'Leary lived out the rest of her life as a virtual recluse, only
leaving her residence to attend daily mass. When she died in 1895,
she was described as 'heartbroken' that she was always blamed for
causing so much destruction.

In 1997, the Chicago City Council passed a resolution exonerating Catherine—and her cow—from all blame.

1903: More than 600 people died when fire broke out at Chicago's recently opened Iroquois Theater. The publishers of Marshall Everett's *The Great Chicago Theater Disaster* wrote in a preface, refer-encing the previous Great Chicago Fire of 1871:

If any good whatever shall come from this second great fire-blast
which has visited the Western Metropolis, it will be the arousal of
the world to a realization of the worthlessness of dead money as
compared with quivering life.

1904: The Great Baltimore Fire, one of the worst city fires in Amer-ican history, destroyed over 1,500 buildings in this Maryland city.

1904: More than 1,000 people died when fire erupted aboard the steamboat *PS General Slocum* in New York's East River; it remained the deadliest individual event in the New York area until 9/11.

1906: An underground fire in a mine at the Courrières, France coal mine triggered a massive explosion causing 1,099 deaths and hundreds of injuries in Europe's worst mining disaster.

1907: The worst mining disaster in U.S. history occurred as at least 361 men and boys died in a coal mine explosion in Monongah, West Virginia.

1912: The British luxury liner *RMS Titanic* sunk in the North Atlantic off Newfoundland on its maiden voyage after it collided with an iceberg at 11:40 pm. The ship went under two and a half hours later, killing over 1,500 people; 710 survived.

1914: The worst mining disaster in Japanese history occurred after a gas explosion at the Mitsubishi Hojyo coal mine in Kyushu, Japan. The blast, which blew elevator cabs nearly 50 feet into the air, affected people within a 200-meter radius of the mine's entrance and killed 687 miners.

1920s-1990: Libby, Montana, was the epicenter of vermiculite mining, and, at one point, provided 80% of the world's supply. Mining operations caused asbestos release, and hundreds of workers and residents died from mesothelioma. While vermiculite itself is not toxic, the mining deposits around Libby contained massive amounts of actinolite and tremolite—both highly toxic forms of asbestos. As a result, nearly 10% of the town's population died from asbestos-related illness, and the people who died weren't always miners—the asbestos fibers that caused health problems are easy to pass on to others.

1930: Fire broke out inside the overcrowded Ohio Penitentiary in Columbus, killing 322 inmates in the deadliest prison disaster in U.S. history.

1932 -1968: Minamata, Japan's Chisso chemical factory released methylmercury into wastewater, tainting fish that were consumed daily by residents. The contamination caused mercury poisoning and neurological damage known asMinamata disease, causing more than 900 deaths. Almost 2,300 victims were identified as having Minamata disease, with more than 10,000 people receiving compensation from the Chisso corporation.

1940: More than 200 people trapped inside a dance hall died in the Rhythm Club Fire in Natchez, Mississippi, one of the deadliest night-club fires in U.S. history.

1942: The world's worst mining death occurred at the Benxihu coal mine in Liaoning Province, China. A mixture of gas and coal dust caused an underground mine to explode. To contain the blaze, authorities closed the ventilation system and the entrance to the mine, suffocating about 1,549 workers.

1943: In London's East End, 173 people died in a crush of bodies at the Bethnal Green Tube station, which was being used as a wartime air raid shelter.

1947: The French cargo ship *S.S. Grandcamp*, carrying over 2,000 tons of ammonium nitrate fertilizer, blew up in the harbor in Texas City, Texas. A nearby ship, the *High Flyer*, which was carrying ammonium nitrate and sulfur, caught fire and exploded the following day. The combined blasts and fires killed nearly 600 people and injured 5,000 in the worst industrial accident in U.S. history. Various estimates place the cost of lost property at roughly $670 million to $1.3 billion today.

1954: An explosion occurred aboard the aircraft carrier *USS Bennington* off Rhode Island, killing 103 sailors.

1955: In motor racing's worst disaster, more than 80 people were killed during the 24 hours of Le Mans in France when two cars collided and crashed into spectators.

1960: The deadliest coal mine disaster since the 1949 founding of the People's Republic of China occurred when a methane explosion at the Laobaidong coal mine near Datong City, China, killed 684 people.

1961: Seventy-three people, including all 18 members of the U.S. figure skating team en route to the World Championship in Czechoslovakia, were killed in the crash of a Sabena Airlines Boeing 707 in Belgium.

1963: In Japan's second-deadliest coal mine disaster, a coal dust explosion at the Mitsui Miike coal mine killed 458 miners and injured 833.

1966: The U.S. Navy recovered a hydrogen bomb that the U.S. Air Force had lost in the Mediterranean Sea off Spain following a B-52 crash.

1966: Described as one of the U.K.'s worst mining incidents, the Welsh Valley village of Aberfa was devastated after an avalanche of mining waste travelled towards the village at speeds between 11 and 21 miles-per-hour in waves up to 30 feet high, resulting in the deaths of 144 people and the destruction of several schools and 18 homes.

1967: On December 15, 1967, the Silver Bridge between Gallipolis, Ohio, and Point Pleasant, West Virginia, collapsed. On that fateful day that refused to be forgotten, the Ohio River claimed the lives of 46 people. Driving over the Silver Bridge, the victims died from drowning and icy waters. The tragedy became the inspiration for Gray Barker's *Silver Bridge* (1970) and John Keel's *Mothman Prophesies* (1975) and a 2002 motion picture of the same name.

1968: East London's Ronan Point disaster was caused by a gas explosion on the 18th floor of the newly constructed 22-story tower block, killing four people and injuring 17 others. The tower was built using a prefabricated kit of concrete parts, a new concept developed after World War II.

1970: Following the passing of the Clean Air Act in the U.S., which restricted the use of leaded gasoline, researchers have tracked the sharp decline of lead in human blood. In the 20th century, lead pollution predominantly came from the emissions of vehicles burning leaded gasoline.

1972: A fire at the Sunshine silver mine in Kellogg, Idaho, claimed the lives of 91 miners who succumbed to carbon monoxide poisoning.

1975: Members of the new Khmer Rouge-led Cambodian government seized an American merchant ship, the *SS Mayaguez*, in international waters, sparking a three-day battle that resulted in the deaths of 41 Americans.

1976: The Seveso accident leaked six tons of toxic chemicals at an industrial plant north of Milan, Italy. The factory was producing 2,4,5-Trichlorophenol, which has been used as a chemical weapon and in weedkillers. Children were hospitalized with skin inflammation, hundreds of residents suffered from skin conditions, and huge areas of land were evacuated. Thousands of animals died or had to be slaughtered to prevent toxins entering the food chain.

1976: The oil tanker *Argo Merchant* broke apart near Nantucket Island off Massachusetts almost a week after running aground, spilling 7.7 million gallons of oil into the North Atlantic.

1979: Three Mile Island, the Pennsylvania nuclear power plant outside Harrisburg, experienced a partial meltdown. Its remaining operational reactor was shut down in 2019 as it became too expensive to operate.

1979: Just after takeoff from Chicago's O'Hare Airport, 273 people died when an American Airlines DC-10 crashed.

1980: Thirty-five people were killed when a freighter rammed the Sunshine Skyway Bridge over Tampa Bay in Florida, causing a 1,300-foot section of the southbound span to collapse.

1981: Fourteen people were killed when a Marine jet crashed onto the flight deck of the aircraft carrier *USS Nimitz* off Florida.

1981: The disaster surrounding the Kansas City Hyatt Regency happened after the fourth-floor elevated walkway collapsed, falling onto another walkway two floors down and eventually into the lounge below, killing 114 people and injuring 200. A faulty design did not meet the minimum safety requirements but had gone unnoticed in the building process, causing the walkway to collapse.

1984: A cloud of methyl isocyanate gas escaped from a pesticide plant operated by a Union Carbide subsidiary in Bhopal, India, causing an estimated 15,000 to 20,000 deaths and more than 500,000 injuries. The accident was caused by malfunctioning safety systems and a runaway pressure increase that leaked 40 tons of methyl isocyanate into the atmosphere.

1985: On June 3, 1985, all 329 people on an Air India Boeing 747 were killed when it crashed into the Atlantic Ocean near Ireland after a bomb planted by Sikh separatists exploded onboard.

1986: A reactor explosion at the Chernobyl Nuclear Power Plant released 400 times more radioactive material than the atomic bomb dropped on Hiroshima, exposing over 5 million residents of Ukraine, Slovakia, and Belarus to radiation. It took nearly two weeks and military intervention to extinguish the fires, and 28 Chernobyl workers died from radiation less than six months after the disaster. Chernobyl represents the world's most infamous man-made nuclear accident. The structure is now covered by a massive steel shelter to contain any radiation leaks, and the government established a 19-mile "exclusion zone."

1989: The supertanker Exxon Valdez ran aground on a reef in Alaska's Prince William Sound and began leaking an estimated 11 million gallons of crude oil.

1993: In less than 10 seconds, Thailand's Royal Plaza Hotel collapsed and "transformed the six-story complex into a pile of rubble," leaving only the front elevator hall. Gradual deformation due to creep weakened all the ground floor support columns, and when one failed, the rest rapidly followed, resulting in one of the worst building collapses in Thailand and the deaths of 137 individuals.

1995: The most devastating building collapse in the history of South Korea resulted in 502 deaths and 937 injuries after an office building was converted into the Sampoong Department Store. Industrial design requirements were ignored as criminal negligence led to structural overload, causing the building to collapse with 1,500 employees inside it.

1996: Eleven people were killed in a fiery collision between an Amtrak passenger train and a Maryland commuter train in Silver Spring, Maryland.

1996: An Atlanta-bound ValuJet DC-9 caught fire shortly after takeoff from Miami and crashed into the Florida Everglades, killing all 110 people on board.

1996: Regarded as the first internet conspiracy of the Cyber Deep State, Trans World Airlines Flight 800 exploded over Long Island, killing all 230 passengers and crew.

2001: On 9/11, two terrorist-hijacked commercial airliners struck the Twin Towers, resulting in the deaths of 2,977 individuals. Constructed in 1973, the towers were comprised of lightweight steel, a central core, and a structured system that supported itself even if one column failed. The towers were designed to bear 5,000 tons of lateral wind load, but 90,000 gallons of burning jet fuel weakened the building, causing the floor slabs to collapse one after another.

2003: A fire sparked by pyrotechnics broke out during a concert by the rock group Great White at the Station nightclub in Rhode Island. 100 people died and over 200 were injured.

2005: A series of explosions at a petrochemical plan in the Chinese city of Jilin released around 110 tons of pollutants into the Songhua River, which supplied drinking water to several large cities. The explosions caused the evacuation of more than 10,000 people.

2006: The world's biggest mud volcano struck Sidoarjo, Indonesia—created by a gas well explosion and drilling by an energy company, although company officials claimed an earthquake around 155 miles away caused the problem.

2009: After declaring an emergency in Libby, Montana, the U.S. government decontaminated more than 3,000 asbestos-plagued sites. More than one million cubic yards of material was replaced, and more than half a billion dollars was spent to decontaminate the town. Hundreds of people died from asbestos-related health issues, thousands more have experienced illness, and new deaths and diseases were still being reported as late as 2018 due to the long-term effects of asbestos fibers. Libby is the biggest asbestos clean-up project in U.S. history.

2010: The Deepwater Horizon oil rig (a floating platform drilling an exploratory oil well around 18,300 feet below sea level) was the largest marine oil spill in history, with 210 million gallons of oil released into the Gulf of Mexico off the coast of Louisiana. The oil flowed for 87 days before being contained almost three months later. A blowout preventer meant to stop this type of accident failed, allowing a surge of methane gas to reach the platform, where it exploded, caught fire, and sank, killing 11 workers. The spill killed marine wildlife, damaged ecosystems, destroyed Gulf Coast jobs dependent on tourism, and induced negative health effects on residents. Further complicating matter, the oil dispersant used in the cleanup also caused damage by permeating the food chain.

2012: A 20-story Rio, Brazil office building crashed into another ten-story building and a smaller building, causing a wave of dust, killing at least 17 people. It is believed that illegal construction renovations weaken the 20-story building, causing it to collapse and bringing down two other smaller buildings.

2013: The Dhaka, Bangladesh garment factory collapse (also referred to as the 2013 Savar building collapse or the Collapse of Rana Plaza) was a structural failure where an eight-story commercial building collapsed. It is considered "the deadliest non-deliberate structural failure accident in modern human history" and "the deadliest garment factory disaster in history," resulting in 1,134 deaths and 2,500 injuries—caused by structural negligence and illegal construction work.

2013: The Justice Department ended its criminal probe of the Deepwater Horizon disaster and Gulf of Mexico oil spill, with a U.S. judge agreeing to let London-based oil giant BP PLC plead guilty to manslaughter charges for the deaths of 11 rig workers and pay a record $4 billion in penalties.

2014: Malaysia Airlines Flight MH370, a Boeing 777 with 239 people on board, vanished during a flight from Kuala Lumpur to Beijing, setting off a massive and ultimately unsuccessful search.

July 17, 2014: Malaysian Airlines Flight MH17 was shot down over eastern Ukraine by Russian forces, killing all 298 passengers and crew.

2015: Germanwings Flight 9525, an Airbus A320, crashed into the French Alps, killing all 150 people on board. Investigators said the jetliner was deliberately downed by the 27-year-old co-pilot, Andreas Lubitz.

2018: California's extreme weather conditions triggered 8,500 wildfires that killed over 100 people, destroyed more than 24,000 buildings and burning 2 million acres of land. Man-made climate change has been blamed for the years that preceded the fires where increasing temperatures and dying trees provided ample fuel for fires to spread.

2022: OxyContin maker Purdue Pharma reached a nationwide settlement over its role in the opioid crisis, with the Sackler family members who own the company boosting their cash contribution to as much as $6 billion in a deal intended to staunch a flood of lawsuits.

2023: The submersible vessel *Titan*, on an expedition to view the wreckage of the *Titanic* in the North Atlantic Ocean, imploded, killing all five people aboard. Among them was Stockton Rush, the American CEO of the tourism and expeditions company OceanGate, who was blamed for not attaining proper certification, arguing that excessive safety protocols and regulations hindered innovation.

2023: On February 3, 2023, a train carrying a toxic mixture of hazardous chemicals jumped the tracks in East Palestine, Ohio, derailing 38 railcars. Several railcars burned for over two days. Emergency crews released hydrogen chloride, vinyl chloride, and phosgene into the air. The "controlled burns" generated a massive black plume of smoke that spread over the area and forced evacuations over health concerns. By October, Norfolk Southern had removed more than 167,000 tons of contaminated soil and more than 39 million gallons of tainted water from the derailment site.

2024: Over 60 cetaceans—an order of aquatic mammals that includes whales and dolphins—have died since fuel oil spilled out of two storm-stricken tankers in the Kerch Strait, near the Russia-occupied Crimean Peninsula. An estimated 200,000 tons of sand and soil were contaminated in what has been called an "ecological disaster."

2024: Oakland, Wisconsin. Roughly 70,000 gallons of oil from a pipeline spilled into the ground in Wisconsin. The problem was discovered November 11 in Jefferson County by an Enbridge Energy technician, the *Milwaukee Journal Sentinel* reported, citing a federal accident report.

2024: Negotiators working on a treaty to address the global crisis of plastic pollution for a week in Busan, South Korea, failed to reach an agreement and plan to resume talks next year. They are at an impasse over whether the treaty should reduce the total plastic on Earth and put global, legally binding controls on toxic chemicals used to make plastics.

2025: Research published in the journal *Nature* warned that nearly a quarter of animals living in freshwater rivers and lakes are threatened with extinction because of contamination. Out of 23,500 species of dragonflies, fish, crabs, and other animals that depend exclusively on freshwater ecosystems, 24% are at risk of extinction due to pollution, dams, water extraction, agriculture, invasive species, climate change, and other disruptions.

14

THE FOUR HORSEMEN OF THE APOCALYPSE

Replete with violence and suffering, the Book of Revelation describes humankind's final gasp in the pink mists of oblivion. Revelation is the New Testament's final book, classified by theologians as "apocalyptic" rather than "historical." It makes extensive use of visions, symbols, and allegory that most scholars believe were written by the Christian prophet John, who called himself a "servant" of Jesus. John wrote that he received his visions while on the island of Patmos, as revealed in Revelation 6:1-8:

> *The Four Horsemen of the Apocalypse were given authority over a fourth of the Earth, to kill with sword and with famine and with pestilence and by wild beasts of the Earth.*

John's vision foretold that the Four Horsemen, having been granted divine authority, will ride in a rolling thunder, bringing about four catastrophic events. They will appear after the opening of the first four of the seven seals, heralding the final cataclysm before the second coming of Christ.

The Four Horsemen of the Apocalypse (1498) by Albrecht Dürer was part of his series of woodcuts illustrating the Biblical prophecies regarding the coming of the Apocalypse. Albrecht Dürer, *CC0, via Wikimedia Commons.*

The Seven Seals

The Seven Seals are essential components of the Book of Revelation, symbolizing God's plan for the end times—seals that can only be broken by Christ "as the Lamb of God." The seals denote some of the Bible's most notable apocalyptic symbols, including: (1) The White Horse. (2) The Red Horse. (3) The Black Horse. (4) The Pale Horse. (5) The Martyrs. (6) Cosmic Disturbances. (7) Silence and the Seven Trumpets.

Schools of eschatology, the branch of theology concerned with the end-time, debate what each seal represents. These schools are separated into two camps, the preterists and the futurists; According to preterist interpretation of Scripture, the Book of Revelation is a symbolic picture of 1st-century conflicts, not a description of what will occur in the end times. All prophecy in the Bible is really history, they say. Still, Christian idealists and futurists believe the seven seals are prophecies of the Last Judgment, connected to modern-day societal ills and the end times.

The Four Horsemen represent two agents of war and one each of famine and pestilence. They are described by biblical scholars in a disconcerting blend of seals, colors, and menace:

I: The First Seal—Rider on White Horse.

As the Savior breaks the first seal of the great book, a wondrous scene flashes before the gaze of the holy apostle John, He says, "And I looked, and behold, a white horse. He who sat on it had a bow; and a crown was given to him, and he went out conquering and to conquer (Revelation 6:2).

The Color—The white horse (Conquest) represents a military conqueror. Its rider (Faithful and True) will ride upon His white horse, and conquer death, famine, disease, and every pestilent thing.

The rider has a bow, representing violence, and wears a crown. White is the emblem of both victory and purity.

Historical Interpretation — (1) The white rider is Christ. (2) The white rider is the antichrist waging a physical and spiritual war. (3) The first horseman was released upon the death of Christ. (4) The seal was broken after the end of Rome's golden age (96–180 CE).

II: The Second Seal—Rider on a Red Horse.

> *When He opened the second seal, I heard the second living creature saying, 'Come and see.' Another horse, fiery red, went out. And it was granted to the one who sat on it to take peace from the earth, and that people should kill one another; and there was given to him a great sword (Revelation 6:3, 4).*

The Color—The fiery red horse (Warfare) depicts fresh blood spilled in battle as it "takes peace from the earth."

Historical Interpretation — (1) Represents the Hundred Years War between England and France, from 1337–1259. (2) Represents the period of instability that engulfed imperial Rome after the death of Marcus Aurelius in 180 CE. (3) Is a personification of the bloodshed that men commit against one another. (4) Prophesized Roman emperors putting Christians to death and destroying copies of the Bible.

III: The Third Seal—Rider on a Black Horse.

> *The third seal was broken, and the apostle says, "When He opened the third seal, I heard the third living creature say, 'Come and see.' So I looked, and behold, a black horse, and he who sat on it had a pair of scales in his hand" (Revelation 6:5, 6).*

The Color—The black horse (Famine and Pestilence) is typically the color of gloom, mourning, and tragedy. Its rider has a pair of scales in his hand and recites the worth of wheat and barley.

Historical Interpretation — (1) The Black Horse represented the Bubonic plague (1346 to 1353), which killed as many as 50 million (perhaps 50% of Europe's 14th-century population). (2) Famine, as depicted in the third seal, broke out during the reign of Claudius (41–54 CE). (3) Foretold that the rich will hoard wealth while others suffer economic hardship.

IV: The Fourth Seal—Rider on a Pale Horse.

This is the vision of dark times: "When He opened the fourth seal, I heard the voice of the fourth living creature saying, 'Come and see.' So I looked, and behold, a pale horse. And the name of him who sat on it was Death, and Hades followed with him. And power was given to them over a fourth of the earth, to kill with sword, with hunger, with death, and by the beasts of the earth." (Revelation 6:7, 8).

The Color—The pale greenish gray horse (Death) resembles the skin of corpses, and is followed by Hades, signifying widespread mortality and a significant loss of life from the combined effects of war, famine, disease, and wild beasts.

The pale horse has the power of famine, plague, and death by the sword and wild beasts (Revelation 6:8.)

Historical Interpretation — (1) Represents The Great Famine of 1315–1317, which caused widespread death and suffering. (2) Represents the persecution and mass murder of Jews in the Roman Empire. (3) Represents the death and suffering that follow war and famine.

V: The Fifth Seal: The Martyrs. The fifth seal reveals the souls of martyrs under the altar and highlights the persecution of believers and their call for divine justice.

And when the Lamb opened the fifth seal, I saw under the altar the souls of those who had been slain for the word of God and for the testimony they had upheld. And they cried out in a loud voice, 'How long, O Lord, holy and true, until You avenge our blood and judge those who dwell upon the earth?' Then each of them was given a white robe and told to rest a little while longer, until the full number of their fellow servants, their brothers, were killed, just as they had been. (Revelation 6:9-11.)

VI: The Sixth Seal: Cosmic Disturbances. The opening of the sixth seal brings about cosmic events that signify the beginning of God's direct intervention in the world.

And when I saw the Lamb open the sixth seal, there was a great earthquake, and the sun became black like sackcloth of goat hair, and the whole moon turned blood red, and the stars of the sky fell to the earth, like unripe figs dropping from a tree shaken by a great wind. The sky receded like a scroll being rolled up, and every mountain and island was moved from its place. (Revelation 6:12-14).

VII: The Seventh Seal: Silence and the Seven Trumpets

When the Lamb opened the seventh seal, there was silence in heaven for about half an hour." This silence precedes the sounding of the seven trumpets, which introduce further judgments upon the earth. (Revelation 8:1.)

Apocalyptic Awe

The Four Horsemen are among the most popular biblical themes. The 15th-century Northern Renaissance artist Albrecht Dürer in his *Four Horsemen of the Apocalypse* (1498) illustrated what Dr. Sally Hickson described as "Sinister apocalyptic cowboys of world-ending destruction." The Horsemen's popularity was again recognized when Spanish writer Vincent Blasco Ibanez (1867–1928) published a book, *The Four Horsemen of the Apocalypse*, in 1916. But those creations are not solely that of an earlier time, or only of interest to academic eschatologists. Hickson claims that American westerns, like Dürer's woodcuts, are "almost all predicated on Christian themes (like the Four Horsemen) and riddled with simple symbolic numbers." Hickson cites such classics as *High Noon* (1952), *The Magnificent Seven* (1960), and *3.10 to Yuma* (2007) as examples of Apocalyptic Awe embracing the past:

> *This is why, for me, Dürer's* Four Horsemen, *drawn from the Book of Revelation (the last book of the New Testament, which tells of the end of the world and the coming of the Kingdom of God), have always been the sinister apocalyptic cowboys of world-ending destruction; Conquest, War, Pestilence (or Famine), and Death itself.*

What goes around comes around, and that which was old is new again. Biblical prophesies of the end times are an integral part of cautionary tales and popular culture. Johnny Cash's late-life classic, The Man Comes Around (2002), begs to be recognized as an essential part of this discussion and as an illustration of how the end times have been assimilated into American cowboy culture and country and folk music. The Book of Revelation, the final book of the Christian Bible, has been repurposed, redefined, and retrofitted for the 21st century. The "Man in Black" said it best.Dürer's *Four Horsemen* illustrated the severity of the tribulation period and the need for repentance. It served as an admonition that we will suffer mightily before we are saved. The Four Horsemen warned of specific doom within a specific time. But lessons learned from a shadowy span of thousands and thousands of years reveal that these catastrophes, like multi-headed hydras, are never ending, created either by the Hand of God or by the arrogance of man.

15

WEAPONIZED RELIGION

The greatest tragedy in mankind's entire history may be the hijacking of morality by organized religion.

— ARTHUR C. CLARK

We are born into fear and then we die. Homer called our finality "The Black Death" and Raymond Chandler called it "The Big Sleep." W.C. Fields referred to it as "The Man in the Bright Nightshirt." Eschatologists are consumed with the end times, a combination of the paranormal and mythological, rightfully seeking comfort from the Word of God. Moses said that God revealed himself in the burning bush. Abraham said that God promised him all the land that he could see, and that the number of his children would rival that of "the dust of the earth." Religious leaders Warren Jeffs, Jim Jones, David Koresh, William Miller, and Joseph Smith claimed that God spoke to them. Peter Sutcliffe, the Yorkshire Ripper, believed that the voice of Jesus instructed him to kill women, and Shoko Asahara declared himself Christ.

All those purported God encounters have been built on towers of contradiction, surrounded by moats of misinterpretation. Scholars and eschatologists debate the meaning of scripture, the Seven Seals, and the Book of Revelation, while secular literature connects the paranormal to the apocalypse. We can find innumerable examples with a few quick keystrokes and precise search words, but the quest is baffling and inconclusive. Nobody has the answers.

Explaining the connection between the paranormal and the apocalypse is like describing a thousand-year-old gnarled cypress tree. It is old and new, living and dying, blanketed in dewy moss, fig buttercups, and thousands of swarming insects. Draped in a majestic beginning and end, it smells of life's richness and death's sweet decay. Like that tree, the paranormal encompasses a spiritual, supernatural, and scientific spectacle of Alpha Omega, of magical osmosis and voices of lost souls. It is Tesla's vibration, frequency and energy, and everything everywhere all at once.

The Fear of Groupthink

Fear is present in modern-day sermons, used by faith healers as a means of subjugation. It can produce a loss of self and mindless conformity, rendering protest and revolt less likely. And while some church leaders preach well-crafted messages of faith and hope, others with hypocritical tongues and fingers of greed amass substantial wealth in a provocative disparity between clergy and flock. Megachurch millionaires and televangelists lavish in exotic mansions and private jets, soliciting donations from people existing near poverty. It is an example of religion as big business—McDonalds, Coca Cola, Kellog's Corn Flakes, and the United Church of Give Me More Money. Fear can be instilled in groups through brainwashing and "groupthink," a psychological phenomenon coercing individuals to conform to the majority opinion without critically evaluating information. Members think as one, senseless lemmings leaping to their deaths in a covenant of blind faith.

Doomsday Cults

There is consolation in numbers. Connecting to a group is one of the greatest human experiences. But joining a social structure gives us the option to participate in either a representative democracy or an authoritarian system. In the former, group deliberation promotes problem-solving and consensus because critical, evidence-based thinking is crucial for maintaining freedom and autonomy. Each citizen has a voice and a vote, a tradition observed in our courtrooms, local school boards, and fire hall meetings.

The opposite pathway invites the threat of demagoguery. This iron-fisted ideology is used by charismatic cult leaders. Eric C. Miller, professor of communication studies at Bloomsburg University of Pennsylvania, has defined demagoguery as "a manipulative form of speech that appeals to fear, anger, and resentment, and directs these emotions toward a vulnerable scapegoat." History's sordid list of demagogues includes Adolph Hitler, Senator Joseph McCarthy, and Southern demagogues, Mississippi Governor Theodore Bilbo and Alabama Governor George Wallace. Miller believes that Donald Trump's name belongs on that list for his scapegoating of minorities and near constant use of white supremacy dog whistles.

Fear is a very effective weapon often used by politicians and religious leaders. The rules are essentially: (1) Fear the future and all things unknown. (2) Assimilate with a group/cult. (3) Relinquish your autonomy. (4) Think and behave like others. (5) Submit to authority. (6) Depend on others for your safety.

Aum Shin Rikyo

Those previously listed rules, along with dread and alienation, drive individuals into the arms of radical movements. Members of the Japanese cult Aum Shin Rikyo (Supreme Truth) were brainwashed into believing that World War III was coming and only its members would survive. The group's founder, Shoko Asahara, declared himself

Christ and the first "enlightened one" since Buddha. Aum Shin Rikyo blended Hindu and Buddhist beliefs with elements of apocalyptic Christian prophesies. The group had attained official status as a Japanese religious organization in 1989, but on March 20, 1995, as millions of Japanese commuters began to shuttle into the Tokyo subway system—one of the world's busiest underground systems—they were attacked by members of Aum Shin Rikyo, using a liquid nerve agent. According to *BBC News*:

> *The toxin struck victims down in a matter of seconds, leaving them choking and vomiting, some blinded and paralyzed. Thirteen people died, and at least 5,800 were injured in five coordinated attacks on three train lines. The cause was Sarin, a nerve agent developed by the Nazis. It was the worst domestic terror attack ever carried out on Japanese soil.*

The cult was suspected of an attack in the city of Matsumoto, in the Japanese Alps, the previous year. For their crimes, 13 members, including Asahara, were sentenced to death.

Branch Davidians

Another self-anointed messiah and fearmonger was David Koresh (aka Vernon Howell), who led the Branch Davidians, a splinter sect of the Seventh Day Adventists. Koresh claimed to have cracked the code of the Seven Seals in the Book of Revelation and said he was the modern-day incarnation of Cyrus, the prophet who liberated the Jews from Babylon. Koresh's sect stockpiled weapons in anticipation of the apocalypse. On April 19, 1993, the Federal Bureau of Alcohol, Tobacco and Firearms used tanks and tear gas to end a 51-day siege of the compound. Koresh (along with about 80 of his followers) was found dead from an apparently self-inflicted gunshot wound to the head—just like Jim Jones 15 years earlier. In *The True Believer* (1951), Eric Hoffer observed a startling common denominator among cult groups:

Though there are obvious differences between the fanatical Christ-
ian, the fanatical Mohammedan, the fanatical nationalist, the
fanatical Communist, and the fanatical Nazi, it is yet true that the
fanaticism which animates them may be viewed and treated as one.

The Manson Family

Cult leader Charles Manson persuaded three of his "Manson Family" to carry out the Tate-La Bianca murders. Victims of this 1969 blood bath included actress Sharon Tate and six other people. Linda and Rod Dubrow-Marshall, writing for *The Conversation*, said that Manson wanted to trigger "Helter Skelter," an apocalyptic race war that would elevate him to a position of world leadership:

The key to Manson's control, as with all cult leaders, was to ensure
that followers not only saw him as an all-powerful, messiah-like
figure, but that followers see themselves as members of a superior
elite that has the answer to the world's problems – even if that
means killing the rest of the world along the way.

Manson was a delusional cultist, a false prophet who controlled his "family" members through sex, drugs, and fear. The Bible's Book of Revelation (13:11–15; 16:13; 19:20; 20:10) warned of the False Prophet enticing us to worship the Antichrist. That warning is still being parroted by charismatic orators who preach apocalyptic fear, uncertainty, and reliance upon messiahs.

Although he was referring to Nazi Germany, novelist Aldous Huxley, in The Olive Tree and other essays, (1947) offered political and social commentary on the rise of Europe's fascism and an explanation as to why individuals submit to violent cults:

We protect our minds by an elaborate system of abstractions, ambi-
guities, metaphors and similes from the reality we do not wish to
know too clearly; we lie to ourselves, in order that we may still have

*the excuse of ignorance, the alibi of stupidity and incomprehension,
possessing which we can continue with a good conscience to commit
and tolerate the most monstrous crimes.*

The War of the Worlds

Warren Steed Jeffs, leader of the Fundamentalist Church of Jesus
Christ of Latter-Day Saints (FLDS), was placed on the FBI's Ten Most
Wanted List for arranging illegal child marriages between adult male
followers and underage girls. The cult leader is believed to have ille-
gally "wed" at least 80 women and girls, whom he called his "spiritual" or "celestial" wives, some as young as 12. Jeffs, whom many
members of the FLDS consider their prophet, repeatedly proclaimed
the end of days and in 2005 issued a warning to his followers:

> *The day of the judgments of God have begun. That day is upon us.
> And the judgements of God have begun with the House of God. And
> that means this is the day of his choosing.*

Jeffs warned that the world would end on April 6, 2005, which is the
date in 1830 when Joseph Smith founded the Church of Jesus Christ
of Latter-day Saints. Some LDS leaders have claimed it is Christ's
true birthday. After Jeff's apocalypse failed to materialize, he
published a book titled *Jesus Christ Message to All Nations* (2012),
warning that retribution will be forthcoming to his enemies.

Often, our personal beliefs are criticized when they do not corre-
spond to those of our peers. Fear of speaking the truth (or searching
for the truth) may force some to forsake their moral compass. *The
Catcher in the Rye* (1951) by J.D. Salinger, a "coming of age" novel, or a
"bildungsroman," was banned over the decades for use of profanity,
sexually explicit content, description of underage drinking and drug
use, and hints of the occult. In 1968, the book was accused of being a
Communist plot. What was it about *Catcher* that created such fear,
when it was only another in a long list of books that described

youthful exploration and curiosity? Was it <u>curiosity</u> that was feared? Did those in power want the "truth" to remain hidden from "vulnerable" eyes justly searching for answers?

Franz Kafka's existential classic, *The Metamorphosis*, (1915), has been interpreted as an allegory for the challenges of maintaining one's individuality in a conformist society. Many forsake their individuality to join a group. It is easier to "go along to get along" and not rock the boat, silently falling on knees, with no tears or emotion, just mindless zombies frozen in fear. They become one of the faceless, voiceless minions who march in lockstep to their leader's drumbeat. Fear forces us to conform like the children who obediently followed the Pied Piper. We are warned to step in line and conform to social, religious, and political ideologies. If we refuse, we will be shunned by societies like early American pilgrims and strict Amish communities, or banished to an infinite number of prisons, such as the Russian Gulag, Rikers Island, or hell itself. But nonconformists and iconoclasts, such as Copernicus, Bruno, and Galileo, have rocked the boat and changed the world with courage and unorthodox theories, sometimes paying the ultimate price. Galileo was placed under house arrest, and Bruno was burned at the stake for his "heretical" ideologies.

In her book, *On Becoming Fearless*, Arianna Huffington issued this warning:

> *If you let them, the hungry little gremlins of compromise will devour your soul bit by bit and come to dominate your life. They feed the fear of being left out, the fear that survival will be impossible outside the tribe. No wonder fear shoots through our veins, constricting our blood flow and shutting down our creative energy— we are in survival mode.*

Fear of Terrorism

Fear of terrorism is a 21st-century reality retraumatizing us through incessant media imagery. Individuals do not have to be physically violated to experience the effects of trauma. A type of collateral damage is suffered by those who witness violence, or as therapist John Bradshaw wrote, "A witness to violence is a victim of violence." Exposure to trauma triggers feelings of fear, helplessness, and horror, and the belief that the future is dangerous.

The worst terrorist attacks in U.S. history occurred on September 11, 2001, when 19 suicide jihadists crashed four U.S. commercial jets—two into the World Trade Center in New York City, one into the Pentagon, and one into a field in Shanksville, Pennsylvania. Those well-organized and well-funded al-Qaida attacks killed nearly 3,000 people, leaving emotional and physical scars that exist to the present day.

Three days before the 2004 general elections in Spain, 10 bombs exploded inside four commuter trains in Madrid. The bombings were one of the deadliest terrorist attacks in Europe's history, killing 193 people and injuring 2,000. The attack was linked to al-Qaida-inspired militants as revenge for Spanish involvement in the Iraq war.

The Arabic word *jihad* means "effort" or "struggle" and can describe: (1) An individual's internal struggle against baser instincts. (2) The struggle to build a righteous Muslim society. (3) A religious war against nonbelievers. It is the latter interpretation that has caused untold global destruction. According to the *Counter Terrorism Guide*:

> *Al-Qa'ida exploits under governed areas, regional conflicts, and local grievances to recruit new members and derive resources. Al-Qa'ida affiliates remain committed to attacking the United States and U.S. interests abroad but have varying degrees of capability and access to these targets. These affiliates use a variety of tactics,*

including conventional assaults, improvised explosive devices, suicide operations a, and kidnappings.

Jihadists divide the world into two realms: (1) The "realm of Islam" (*dar al-Islam*), where lands under Muslim rule and Sharia law prevail. (2) The "realm of war" (*dar al-harb*), when war in defense of Islam can be declared in countries not governed by Muslim rule. Legitimate targets (they claim) are those who have abandoned the Sharia instructions and are outside *dar al-Islam*. Iran's Ayatollah Khomeini issued a *fatwa* calling on Muslims to kill Salman Rushdie, author of *The Satanic Verses* (1988), a novel condemned by the Ayatollah as blasphemous against Islam. Rushdie, who spent years in hiding after Khomeini called for his death, was stabbed on a lecture stage, blinding him in one eye and leaving the author with lasting nerve damage. Rushdie's current book, *The Eleventh Hour* (2025) "explores the eternal mysteries of the eleventh hour of life," a name hinting at the apocalypse.

Millenarian concerns about the end of the world have plagued us since ancient times. It has continued with modern-day threats of nuclear war, pandemics, and further trepidations about terrorism, global warming, and the horrible realities of nuclear winter (like the Cretaceous-Paleogene extinction event 66 million years ago that caused the die-off of non-avian dinosaurs) that are both feared and anticipated.

Each of us search for the holy trifecta of meaning, purpose, and belonging, a shared quest expounded by Herman Hesse's *Sidhartha* (1922) and Joseph Campbell's extraordinary and insightful *The Power of Myth* (1988). As told in the Bible's Prodigal Son, this search celebrates those "who once were lost but now have been found." It is the essence of human curiosity, reinforcing our need to climb mountains and discover holy grails. As the Bard of Avon wrote, "therein lies the rub."

The eyes are the windows to the soul. Some see the world through eyes filled with wonder, and others look through eyes of fright. Our view can be represented by a glass that is half full or half empty. Nonbelievers will grasp the glass that is half empty as they look upon dead, stilled waters. They will *scream in horror, with no* sentiment or reverence. They have no joy. Punishment is their calling.

Still others firmly hold onto a glass that is half full as they walk into the sunshine with wide eyes. They dream of being rewarded in a paradise with rivers of milk and honey and never-ending sunsets. For them, life is filled with awe, music, and compassion. Joy, not fear, is their entitlement. Any religion that nurtures that entitlement holds the key to the life we have been promised and is the religion we should embrace.

16

THE LATE GREAT HAL LINDSEY

Then the Lord said to me, "Do not pray for the well-being of this people. Although they fast, I will not listen to their cry; though they offer burnt offerings and grain offerings, I will not accept them. Instead, I will destroy them with the sword, famine, and plague.

— JEREMIAH 14:11-16:15

With larger brains and DNA driving us to understand the unknown, humans have a hunger to invent, problem solve, and "go where no man has gone before." We seek knowledge and completion in a world of real-life crossword and Sudoku puzzles. That hunger has been cleverly exploited in a bizarre example of apocalyptic consumerism, offering recreational "fortune telling" for a dime.

Fortune Teller Machines—rusted hulks littering the boardwalks and amusement parks of yesterday's penny arcades, can still be seen throughout the world. Although Zoltar was the undisputed master of the machines, Madame Zita, Estrella, and Princess Doraldina were equally popular. When offered a coin, these genie machines came to life with flashing eyes, chattering teeth, and turning their heads, before granting fortune card and horoscope predictions. And all this for only a dime.

American astrologer, clairvoyant, and psychic, Jeane Dixon, shared in that need to know. In 1971, after studying the biblical books Daniel, Ezekiel, and Revelations, Dixon predicted the world would end in the year 2037. Dixon, like other messengers of doom, stared down at the swirling tea leaves, looking not for the light, but for the dark. Dixon eagerly followed in the footsteps of another modern-day prophet, one who had captured the pulse of the nation, amassing a cult of worshippers.

Era of the Antichrist

Hal Lindsey became the apocalypse's most prominent voice. The *New York Times* named his *The Late, Great Planet Earth* (1970) the nonfiction book of the 1970s. It sold over 28 million copies and was adapted into a 1978 film by Rolf Forsberg and Robert Amram and narrated by the legendary Orson Welles. Lindsey assumed the role of apocalyptic spokesperson, appearing on primetime television specials that drew an audience of 17 million. Lindsey had secrets to reveal, and people wanted to know what they were.

The Late Great Planet Earth was published by Bantam and featured cover art suggesting that the 1970s were the Era of the Antichrist. They forcefully promoted the book as "a penetrating look at incredible ancient prophecies involving this generation." The book's success was based on five crucial elements: (1) Lindsey used a simplistic, easy-to-understand writing style. (2) People were fascinated with his doomsday predictions. (3) By combining biblical prophecy and political events, a wider audience, including evangelicals and fundamentalists, were reached. (4) The book renewed interest in modern-day connections to biblical prophecy. (5) It was the first Christian prophecy book to be published (and successfully marketed) by a secular publisher.

Baba Vanga: Baba Venga the blind "Nostradamus of the Balkans," predicted that that aliens would help civilization live underwater by 2130, but that Earth would declare war against Mars in 3005.

Eschatologists, both preterists (who believe the end times have already occurred) and futurists (who believe they are still to come), focus on the day after tomorrow. Hal Lindsey was firmly in the latter camp, swiftly ordained as spokesperson for the apocalypse's silent majority. To be clear, he was the only one cornering the market. Eschatological "theologians" like Lindsey focus on the end times, a time of suffering, and of cataclysmic events. Lindsey argued that the establishment of Israel in 1948, and its subsequent military actions, signaled the beginning of the world's end. He posited that a series of conflicts involving Israel, Russia, and an Arab alliance will lead to a confrontation that will bring "unfulfilled prophecies" soon be revealed. After destroying a rebellion by Satan's unbelievers, Christ would establish a "new heaven and new earth." Not everyone bought into his prophesies. After Lindsey's death at 95, ex-Christian writer Captain Cassidy charged that he:

> *[...] grifted his way through life by selling worried Christian normies doom-and-gloom end times prophecies that never, ever came true. Indeed, Hal Lindsey might be almost single-handedly responsible for the entire end times prophecy fad that swept through evangelicalism between the 1970s and the 2010s.*

Lindsey was either a modern-day Nostradamus or a slick huckster who tapped into a vulnerable cult looking to bask in the promise of the afterlife. As he foresaw how history would end, Lindsey discovered that prophesy and religious fear equated to a nice payday. As writer Cassidy concluded, "None of his prophecies about the end times had ever come true." Still, it seems almost impossible to look at current events and not connect them to an apocalyptic scenario, an uncertainty that was key to Lindsey's popularity.

Lindsey wasn't the only one making predictions. Baba Venga (1911–1996), the blind "Nostradamus of the Balkans," made hundreds of predictions during her 50-year career. Baba predicted that a nuclear war between 2010 and 2016 would lead to the abandonment of Europe, warning that Muslims would invade Europe in a "great Muslim war," which would end with Rome being established as the epicenter of an Islamic caliphate. Baba then looked into outer space, predicting that aliens would help civilization live underwater by 2130, but that Earth would declare war against Mars in 3005. The clairvoyant believed her psychic gifts had something to do with "the presence of invisible creatures":

*This gift is given to me by God! He took my human eyesight away,
but he gave me other eyes with which I can see the whole visible
and invisible world. I started helping all other people that were
suffering and became their support and hope.*

Although many of her predictions seemed too fantastic to be authentic, she accurately predicted the September 11 terrorist attacks, the election of Barack Obama as president, and the Brexit vote. But according to Joey Esposito, writing for the premier debunker, *Snopes*:

*Much like with Nostradamus, however, these predictions are vague
at best, and there is no hard evidence proving she even made them
in the first place, only hearsay. Therefore, we have rated this claim
as unfounded.*

Nonetheless, Lisa Trank observed, "One path to understanding (Baba Venga's) mysterious influence is to explore our eternal fascination with future-telling and the paranormal." The paranormal and apocalyptic are essential parts of one another, bridging the faithful to distant worlds. Over 100,000 people visited Baba seeking her talents as a psychic healer. A 2018 study by the Trend marketing and research center found that 75% of Bulgarians believed in her "powers." Georgi Lozanov, a Bulgarian professor of psychiatry and founder of the Institute of Suggestology, conducted extensive research on Baba's predictions and rated her accuracy at a remarkable 85%.

Major Religions

All four major religions have predicted the supposed end times: (1) Christianity's Book of Revelations speaks of the Second Coming and the final judgment. The Book of Daniel is the earliest example of a Jewish Apocalypse, and the most comprehensive is the Book of Enoch. Other texts include the first chapter of the Greek Apocalypse of Baruch, the Syriac Apocalypse, and the Slavonic Book of Enoch. (2) The Hadith describes Islam's Day of Judgment (*Yawm al-Qiyamah*), when the dead will be resurrected and judged by Allah. (3) Hinduism's concept of *Kali Yuga* represents a period of moral decline, leading to eventual renewal through divine intervention. (4) Buddhism focuses on cycles of birth, death, and rebirth (*samsara*), emphasizing personal enlightenment and liberation, rather than apocalyptic events suffering.

Judeo-Christian texts have compiled a listing of mystics possessing special powers, as well as ancient prophets who spoke on behalf of God. These prophets were venerated to the point of being allowed to preach in the temples and ranked second only to the apostles by Paul. Among them were Isaiah, Ezekiel, Daniel, Jeremiah, Abraham, and Moses. Although the 18th-century oracle Mari advised the Assyrian king, Hebrew prophets were obedient to Yahweh, the lawgiver, and not to the king.

The ancient Grecian Delphic oracle is believed to have forecast outcomes of wars and political actions, and, for centuries, modern-day seers have forecasted the end of the world. Joseph Smith, founder of the Mormon church, spoke to God, learning that Jesus would return within the next 56 years. David Berg, the leader of the Children of God, predicted that the comet Kohoutek would create a colossal doomsday event. Internet pastor Paul Begley said that God spoke to him and warned that the blood moon eclipse was a sign of the end times. It was Baptist preacher William Miller's voice that resonated far above the rest. Miller, the head of the Christian Millerite movement, prophesized that the Second Coming would occur in 1844. Miller meticulously calculated the exact date using numerology. The Day of Judgment, he said, would take place on April 18, 1844. Thousands of his followers, feeling the collar of fear, anticipated being cast into the fire, but, Miller preached, this would be a good thing. The Last Judgement would cleanse the world of sin and make the world whole.

Many faithful (estimates vary between 50,000 and 500,000) sold their homes and gave away their jewelry and livestock. But, when this "last day" came and went, Miller told his followers that he'd miscalculated by seven months and that the Apocalypse would now be on October 22, 1844. Once again, Miller's followers climbed hills and rooftops to await ascension. But the reality that unfolded was unexpected. The sun rose and set, and after the day passed without event, one of Miller's followers wrote of the pain:

> *I waited all Tuesday [October 22], and dear Jesus did not come; I waited all the forenoon of Wednesday and was well in body as I ever was, but after 12 o'clock, I began to feel faint, and before dark, I needed someone to help me up to my chamber, as my natural strength was leaving me very fast. I lay prostrate for two days without any pain—sick with disappointment.*

Their leader had deceived them into believing something that mocked their loyalty and faith. There would be no singing praises to the Lord or begging for God's mercy. The congregants experienced a collective sadness, as Millerite Hiram Edson wrote:

> *Our fondest hopes and expectations were blasted, and such a spirit of weeping came over us as I had never experienced before. We wept, and wept, till the day dawn.*

After the sect disbanded, newspapers dramatized its downfall, reporting alleged cases of insanity and suicide. But among the Millerites, their words spoke of expended joy and self-loathing. Miller's prophecies of a spiritual cleansing were hollow words. A 16-year-old Millerite girl, Ellen White, reflected:

> *It was hard to take up the vexing cares of life that we thought had been laid down forever. A bitter disappointment fell upon the little flock whose faith had been so strong, and hope had been so high.*

It was a bitter letdown. Some wanted to embrace the end times, feel God's wrath, and die. Chaos erupted. One Millerite church in Ithaca,

New York, was burned to the ground. A group of Millerites were tarred and feathered in Toronto. Another Millerite group in Illinois was attacked with clubs and knives. The Millerites were left disillusioned. The expected damnation reverberated and it seemed that even the dead trembled in their graves.

In *Psychology Today*, Ewan Morrison asks, "Why would some people be so absorbed by the idea of the Apocalypse that when it fails to occur, they sink into despair?" Morrison believes that some develop a psychological dependence on anticipating the doom of the Apocalypse:

> *This is illustrated by the fact that so many Millerites suffered from what must have been cognitive dissonance after their great disappointment and, unable to admit that they'd been wrong, they went on to invest in new apocalypse date predictions—and so the Advent Christian Church and the Seven Day Adventist sects were born.*

Morrison asserts that some might gain fulfillment in death, as opposed to a life without any guiding structure, or what he calls "a life of meaningless fragments that is itself a 'great disappointment.'" The life one chooses can be filled with fulfillment and joy, but if consisting of Morrison's "meaningless fragments," it will swell with disappointment. The pathway will be uncertain for those who choose to follow fellow lemmings who look over their shoulders, smile, and leap over the ledge. *The God Delusion* (2006), written by Richard Dawkins, understood the relationship between vulnerable children and religious indoctrination:

> *In more recent times, James Dobson, founder of today's infamous 'Focus on the Family' movement, is equally acquainted with the principle: 'Those who control what young people are taught, and what they experience—what they see, hear, think, and believe— will determine the future course for the nation.'*

Although Dawkins was referring specifically to blissfully unaware children, that gullibility can also be applied to docile and undemanding adults. It is easier to follow than to lead, but perilous to allow others to think for us. Kept imprisoned in fear, both children and adults are susceptible to charismatic individuals like William Miller, David Koresh, and James Dobson.

Humankind shares a covenant with seers who supposedly read the stars, interpret dreams, predict births and deaths, and foretell famines, floods, and plagues. Throughout antiquity, sooth-sayers have stood shoulder to shoulder, like tiny soldiers in tin boxes, embracing the religious and secular. "Prophets" like Baba Vanga, Nostradamus, Edgar Cayce, William Miller, and Hal Lindsey, and rusted penny arcade fortune teller machines, have all shouted out the same message, telling us exactly what we wanted to hear.

But while some religious leaders like David Berg, Paul Begley, and William Miller claim to have spoken directly to God, others assert that they *are* the Messiah—a horrifying reality that will be explored next.

Question: Why were authors Erick Von Daniken and Hal Lindsey so incredibly popular and successful with everyday citizens?

17

THE JONESTOWN MASSACRE

Often referred to as the "American Apocalypse," the Jonestown Massacre was one of the worst mass killings in American history. It was perpetrated by Reverend Jim Jones, who compared himself to Jesus Christ and predicted when the world would end.

"Religion is the opiate of the masses," is remembered as Karl Marx's timeless quote. Combined with elements of fear, Marx believed that religion was an effective tool to numb our spirit and control our minds. Much earlier, Seneca the Younger (c.4 BCE–65 CE) discerned, "Religion is regarded by the common people as true, by the wise as false, and by the rulers as useful." Religion offers faith and hope while maintaining a tight rein of control.

But the human spirit is remarkable. Armed with resilience and cognition, it lifts us above mere survival, riding past the unknown realms of darkness. But for some, that human spirit is systematically beaten down in a terrible playbook crafted by religious cult leaders such as David Koresh, Warren Jeffs, and Reverand Jim Jones.

James Warren Jones (1931–1978), the self-proclaimed Jonestown Messiah, was a white minister and a civil-rights activist. He ran his predominantly Black congregation, the Peoples Temple of the Disciples of Christ, with a "fire and brimstone" iron fist. During the 1950s, Jones made trips to Philadelphia, where he was inspired by Father Divine (1876–1965), a charismatic Black preacher and follower of the controversial Black separatist leader Marcus Garvey. Divine founded the International Peace Mission movement and became an important social reformer and champion of racial equality. He was among the pioneers of the of the civil rights movement.

Rev. Jim Jones perpetrated the Jonestown Massacre, one of the worst mass killings in American history. Jones compared himself to Jesus Christ and predicted when the world would end.

Jones began to imitate Divine, creating an integrated family and congregation, transforming his sermons into flamboyant theatrical presentations mixing Pentecostalism and Methodism. Adopting Father Divine's techniques, Jones would move beyond the parameters of Christianity, portraying himself as a prophet and deity. His personality and oratory talent appealed to the Black congregants. James R. Coffey's article, *The Reverend Jim Jones: Profile of a Megalomaniac,* viewed him as "charisma personified" with a natural gift of persuasion:

> *Part showman, part con artist, part huckster, people found it impossible to resist him. And once he set his sights on something cr someone, he was rarely dissuaded. His ability to make the seemingly impossible possible added to his perceived charisma and power. Power, he convinced those around him was divine.*

Jones could skillfully recite entire sections of the Bible. He was smooth-talking, handsome, and riveting. At 5'8", he presented a commanding persona with sunglasses, sideburns, and dusky complexion. Jones was eager to help others in his congregation, and there are numerous accounts of his charity and goodwill, especially within the disadvantaged Black community. Still, during those trying times, the group also experienced racial ostracism and death threats.

Jones claimed his dark hair and high cheekbones came from his mother's Cherokee blood. Growing up in Indiana, Jones was the only child of James Thurman Jones (1887–1951), an older disabled veteran, and Lynetta Putnam Jones (1902–1977), a working mother who believed she was a child of Christ. "My Indian spirit has certain acumen that you won't be able to find anywhere," he said in 1973, lecturing his followers. His adopted multi-racial children were Korean, and his son, Jim Jones, Jr., was Black. According to *PBS:*

> *He and his wife were the first white couple to adopt a Black baby in the state in 1961, the year Freedom Riders trying to desegregate interstate buses were brutally attacked in Alabama. Anonymous threats targeted the Jones family, and they received notes stating that people were praying for the death of their Black son.*

Seeking a more hospitable location, in 1965, the Peoples Temple moved from Indiana to Ukiah, California, a small town about 200 miles north of San Francisco. Peoples Temple member Gary Lambrev remembered:

> *Jim always pointed out not only that his family, his immediate family, was interracial by adoption but that he personally was a man who was profoundly blended of many different racial and ethnic streams. But then increasingly as the organization became blacker and blacker, he began to talk about himself as a Black man, first a man of color, and then a Black man.*

Although he espoused visions of racial and class equality, he lived during an era of segregation and the assassinations of Robert Kennedy and Martin Luther King, the Easter race riots, and the Chicago Democratic Convention police action—all of which were threatening to unravel American society. Something had to break. Jones portrayed the United States as *Babylon* and warned of the Apocalypse. "Race and class warfare will engulf a society trapped in its own hypocrisy," he preached, insisting that "divine socialism" would lead the new world order, once the current one destroyed itself.

Expressing increased paranoia, Jones predicted that a nuclear attack would annihilate the country in 1967. After reading an article in *Esquire* magazine (1962) listing South America as the safest place to survive a thermonuclear blast, he traveled to Guyana and spoke with authorities about establishing his church there. In the 1970s, he moved with some thousand followers to the Jonestown settlement in the South American nation, where he promised to create a utopian community, but, according to *History.com*, Jones' relocation came only after negative media attention and mounting investigations:

> *Negative reports began to surface about the man referred to as "Father" by his followers. Former members described being forced to give up their belongings, homes, and even custody of their children.*

> *They told of being subjected to beatings and said Jones staged fake "cancer healings."*

Socialist Paradise

In December of 1974, the first followers of the Peoples Temple arrived in what would become Jonestown's "socialist paradise." Located on the coast of South America, the English-speaking Guyana had a socialist government and a predominately Black population. Jones described his Guyana retreat as a communal paradise rich with food, where there were no mosquitoes or snakes, and where temperatures hovered around a perfect 72 degrees every single day. But it was all a lie. Arrivals found that the promised "paradise" consisted of only a few huts surrounded by endless and sweltering tropical jungle. Julia Scheeres, author of *A Thousand Lives: The Untold Story of Hope, Deception and Survival at Jonestown* (2011), after inspecting thousands of pages of letters and journals released by the FBI, concluded that the people were starving because the thin jungle soil couldn't grow food:

> *Every day, they are getting up at the break of dawn and going out to the fields to work. During the dry season they do bucket brigades to water the plants, so they don't die. It's back-breaking work and there's no free time—and that's on purpose. Jones knows people are unhappy; there's not enough food, they're separated from their families, it's hot. It's nothing like he promised.*

Members were kept alive on starvation diets and poor-tasting meals of rice-like gruel, with no meat or fish and few fruits and vegetables. Temple members had to forfeit their passports and were forced to work sunup to sundown, constantly reminded that an act of "revolutionary suicide" was preferable to being murdered for their religious convictions. They were programed to believe that Father Jim was "God," and that socialism and "revolutionary suicide" were their destiny. That destiny of suicide and mass killings was prophesied by Jones during a sermon, two years earlier:

I love socialism, and I'm willing to die to bring it about, but if I did,
I'd take a thousand with me.

Impending Capitalist Apocalypse

Addicted to drugs, Jones had become increasingly paranoid and was in declining mental health. He often wore dark sunglasses and traveled with bodyguards. Jones began to preach of an "impending capitalist apocalypse," concepts far removed from his former Pentecostal beliefs. He warned that during the Last Judgment, the world would end in an apocalyptic race war, destroying all non-believers. Only the faithful, and Father Jones, their redeemer, would survive. Cult leaders like Jones set their trap through parables of false hope. They promise a utopian society of peace and harmony, of respect and equality, but, as their disillusioned followers seek refuge from the failed Capitalistic dream, they are forced to step in line, submit, and surrender their freedom, as identified by Christian psychotherapist Alan Loy McGinnis (1933–2005):

> *Unscrupulous salespeople or demagogues like Jim Jones have been*
> *able to persuade persons to do demonic things with the consistency*
> *principle. First, they get a small commitment from someone. Then*
> *they ask for increasingly extreme actions, all in the name of*
> *consistency.*

Although viewed as a messiah, Jones was a slave master whose persuasion included brainwashing and mind control. The TV program, *Crime Investigation* determined that Jones was able "to turn a healthy, happy and normal Christian congregation into a brainwashed mob almost incapable of independent thought."

Like other totalitarians throughout history, Jim Jones demanded a fidelity of God-like obedience, ordering his believers to submit to his authority and acknowledge his sovereignty over their lives. Leslie Kennedy, *History's* website writer, noted:

Jones enforced a rule that when his voice was played over the PA system rigged throughout the commune, no one was allowed to talk.

Drug abuse hijacked Jones' mentality and gradually consumed him. At some predictable juncture, it became an addiction. There were other elements as well: sociopathy, narcissism, and a need for control. But it was methamphetamine, a powerful neural-toxic stimulant, that gave him perceived superpowers, and, in a delusional state, he could stay up for days, hallucinating and ranting to his followers.

Meth also gave Jones delusions of grandeur. He believed he was superhuman and could predict the future. His numerous predictions were not as genuine as those of Nostradamus or Edgar Cayce but fraudulent like those of Charles Dawson and Madam Blavatsky. And although his predictions were numerous, only one—the one representing the Jonestown killing field that, even today, boggles the mind with savage incongruity, came true. How could that have happened? At what point does an individual step in line and place his head on the blood-stained chopping block? Or allow his children and spouses to be murdered or commit suicide? Why and how, we ask.

To be clear, Reverand Jim Jones was a false messiah and pathogen. In clinical terms, he was a psychopath, feeling no remorse for others and receiving sexual gratification from inflicting pain. Still, in the beginning, his congregation practiced Christian virtues and was actively involved in making positive social change and carrying out the message of Jesus—before Jones denounced the Bible and pronounced himself the divine source of truth.

Extended Care Unit

Temple members who were verbally critical of Jones were confined to the "Extended Care Unit" and heavily sedated with barbiturates like quaaludes. Author Jeff Guinn's *The Road to Jonestown: Jim Jones and the Peoples Temple* (2017) addressed Jones' long-time drug addiction and how he used substances as a tool of control:

Jones—who forbade recreational drug use among his followers—took amphetamines and tranquilizers, in both pill and liquid form, to provide significant boosts of energy, or else slow down his racing imagination and allow him to rest. But the amphetamines contributed to Jones' paranoia, and he started to believe the CIA and FBI were tapping the church's phones with plans to infiltrate the Temple with undercover spies.

Jonestown's paradise ended, not in schoolyard practice drills, but in vats of green Kool Aid and pointed guns. The Jonestown Massacre occurred on November 18, 1978, when 909 cult members died in mass murder-suicide. The ending was horrible, with screams of fear and pleas for mercy resonating in the Guianan heat. The youngest members were the first to die. Parents and nurses used syringes to drop a potent mix of cyanide, sedatives, and powdered fruit juice into the children's throats. Adults then lined up to drink the concoction while armed guards surrounded the pavilion.

Jones ordered his followers to drink a flavored, Kool-Aid-like beverage called Flavor Aid, blended with cyanide and the sedatives Valium, chloral hydrate, and Phenergan. They remained childishly optimistic in their love and naivety, even after years of mind control, Scheeres said:

People think they willingly died, but Jones gave them no choice. They were surrounded by a row of guards with crossbows, and then behind them there was another line of guards pointing guns. Meanwhile, Jones is exhorting them to come up and drink this potion to take them to the other side. So, living was never an alternative on that last night. Most people chose to die with their families, and if they didn't drink it, there were many who were injected with the poison.

Jackie Speier's Undaunted: Surviving Jonestown, Summoning

Courage, and Fighting Back (2018) shared her ordeal under the fist of Father Jim.

Cult leaders have a pattern. They're charismatic, paranoid, megalo-maniac. Over time, they control their followers through physical, mental, and emotional abuse, leaving them unable to think inde-pendently. It's not about policy; it's about devotion. These leaders make you believe that they—and only they—have the answers. That's when critical thinking stops and blind obedience begins.

Speier was only 28 when she joined Congressman Leo Ryan's delega-tion to rescue defectors from the Peoples Temple. Ryan and four others were killed by Jones' soldiers. Speier was shot five times at point-blank range. The former congresswoman would spend decades warning about the dangers of unchecked power, blind loyalty, and charismatic manipulation, as embodied by charismatic despots. Few realized the extent of Jones' wickedness. Members of his cult were brainwashed with fear and kept continuously unbalanced and anxious. *Crime Investigation* summed up the depravity of this psychopath:

He would terrorize and beat children in front of their parents, take away men's wives to have sex with them, electroshock elderly folk and force people to drink their own urine and eat their own vomit. The man knew no depths and would do anything to chastise, intim-idate and control his followers...

While "drinking the Kool Aid" has become a sick cultural punch line, Jonestown remains a cautionary tale about religious fanaticism and blind faith. Before the September 11, 2001 terrorist attacks, the tragedy at Jonestown was the worst loss of U.S. civilian lives in a non-natural disaster. Dr. Philip G. Zimbardo, former professor emeritus of psychology at Stanford University, observed:

We will never fully know the truth about what really happened on that fateful day. However, it is vital that we learn and appreciate how it could happen then, and maybe again in our times.

In hindsight, Jonestown never should have happened, because humans have the capacity for rational thought and precious God-given autonomy. We do not have to follow the crowd. We can think for ourselves. Unfortunately, knowing human nature, Jonestown could happen again.

Addicted to power and drugs, Jones embraced Aleister Crowley's hedonist doctrine, "Do what thou wilt shall be the whole of the Law," preaching lessons from the Bible and indulging in the pleasures of the flesh. Jones was heterosexual, homosexual, sadistic, and most likely, in the secret confines of his chambers, masochistic as well.

Although much has been written about how this crazed megalomaniac exerted control over his followers, few have asked why he betrayed his Christian beliefs and his self-proclaimed walk with the Lord. As his Peoples Temple members starved, Jones was sending millions of dollars to secret bank accounts in Panama and Switzerland. The Guyanese military found him on the pavilion stage, dead from a gunshot to the head. With elitist condescension, he cowardly refused to drink the cyanide that he forced on his congregation.

Question: Why was Jonestown known as the American Apocalypse?

18

Y2K AND THE GOD PARTICLE

B uried deep beneath an underground 17-mile ring, running through Switzerland and France, Fermilab's Large Hadron Collider (LHC) holds the promise of answering questions about the nature of the universe, including why the universe consists of matter and not anti-matter. On July 2, 2012, Fermilab teams believed that they discovered The Higgs bosom, erroneously called the "God particle" and considered the Holy Grail of physics. According to the researchers, existence of the "Higgs boson" was highly likely—with a confidence of over 99.9%.

But some physicists warned of the possibility for global destruction, fearing that the LHC could create microscopic black holes, spawned by the powerful crash of subatomic particles. Black holes and "strangelets"—small particles barely the size of a pea—could deflate the Earth in a matter of seconds, and simultaneously choke and collapse the entire planet rendering it a lump of dead matter. As observed by John Loeffler:

This "strange matter" as it would come to be called would quickly convert all normal matter on Earth to strange matter like itself in mere moments, a kind of particle zombie apocalypse powered by exponential growth that would leave the Earth and all life on it reduced to a relatively tiny ball of quarks *about 100 meters across.*

Interesting Science proposed that the panic over strangelets emphasized our fear of a microscopic black hole dragging planet Earth and all of us into the apocalyptic void:

As we approach similar fears about new technologies and an uncertain future, there are lessons to be learned from the strangelet panic and how physicists managed to educate a distrustful public and advance the cause of human understanding.

Ben Kilminster, a scientist at the Collider Detector at Fermilab (CDF) called Tevatron "more than a machine. It's a living creature that has the superhuman ability to see the microscopic quantum world."

Unknown Monstrosities

Tevatron represents the human need to explore and define the gray areas of the unknown—a unique trait embedded within the molecular structure of our DNA and shared with our spirit guides and ancestors. Burning curiosity drives us to search for what is missing and to solve the mystery. It is the single most important essence of being human. But what if we strayed from our pathway, lost in a maze of swamplands and stalked by unknown monstrosities?

Technology is a double-edged sword with divergent pros and cons. Some of it is good, and some is not so good. Looking at the latter, there is little doubt that AI has fostered a culture of fear, fueled by science fiction movies such as *I, Robot,* (2004), *2001 A Space Odyssey* (1968), and *The Terminator* (1984), and by anonymous 21st-century luddites, who, like Chicken Little, scream that the sky is falling. These doom mongers drive individuals away from community and into solitary existence, focusing not on the present but on a dreadful future.

The use of AI is causing anxiety in every corner of industrialized civilization. In 2024, OFF Radio in Krakow, Poland, replaced its journalists with virtual characters created by AI. But after widespread outcries, the radio station ended its experiment with digital intelligence. The station explained the goal had been to inspire a debate about AI, and that it succeeded.

Debates were ignited in both religious and secular quarters. Pope Francis issued a Vatican encyclical (the most authoritative form of papal teaching) in October 2024, warning that consumer-driven societies are being "bombarded by technology." The Pope said we are being disrupted by AI and risk losing a tranquil and patient "interior life." He noted that sophisticated algorithms secretly track our materialistic wants and desires:

> *Our thoughts and will are much more 'uniform' than we had previously thought. They are easily predictable and thus capable of being manipulated. In an era of artificial intelligence, 'we cannot forget that poetry and love are necessary to save our humanity.'*

Technological Horror

Pope Francis' (1936–2025) unexpected warning elevated the debate, but, nonetheless, doomsday scenarios reside in the eye of the beholder. The infamous Y2K bug, predicted to emerge at the turn of the millennium, was a technological horror many feared would create global bedlam when computers transitioned from 1999 to 2000.

But fear has strange bedfellows. A cadre of fundamentalist Christian leaders inflamed anxieties that apocalyptic prophecies were coming true and that the end times were near. *The New York Times* reported one such example of doom mongering:

The Rev. Jerry Falwell suggested that Y2K would be the confirmation of Christian prophecy — God's instrument to shake this nation, to humble this nation. The Y2K crisis might incite a worldwide revival that would lead to the rapture of the church. Along with many survivalists, Mr. Falwell advised stocking up on food and guns.

Steve Hewitt, an ordained Southern Baptist minister and founder of the *Christian Computing Magazine*, said there is a lot more than doom mongering going on, and told the *Deseret News'* Betsy Hart:

A lot of the more extreme evangelical folks have a political agenda —they'd like to see the government fall apart and so, they hope, usher in Christ's reign. For others, the cold truth is that preaching chaos is profitable, and calm doesn't sell many tapes or books.

Because opportunity seldom strikes twice, the cunning Jerry Falwell, as an example, began hawking videos titled *A Christian's Guide to the Millennium Bug*, at $28.00 a copy and sold through his Old-Time Gospel Hour program. Falwell even hawked a line of expensive canned goods called SafeTrek Foods through the *National Liberty Journal* tabloid. Christian writer Rob Boston, in the revealing *False Prophets, Real Profits*, investigated the evangelical hysteria that turned "fears into gold" and God's wrath into opportunities to make money:

Most major Religious Right figures were swept up by the Y2K hysteria, among them Ed Dobson, the Rev. Jerry Falwell, TV preacher D. James Kennedy, leaders of the Promise Keepers, religious broadcaster Pat Robertson and popular evangelical author Tim LaHaye.

A good time was had by all. A handful of prominent Christian ministries racked up sizable profits through fears of the impending Y2K and by selling merchandise such as preparation kits, generators, survival guides, and end-times prophecies. Fear and money went hand in hand. The flames were being fanned and, by late 1999, most institutions were preparing for the worst. *The Guardian*'s Tom Faber charged that the global media reveled "in fantasies of apocalyptic doomsday scenarios," almost like inciting a riot:

> *Articles in* Time *magazine and* Vanity Fair *painted a picture of a Y2K midnight moment, when planes would fall out of the sky, people's savings would be wiped out in the blink of a cursor, home appliances would explode, and nuclear reactors would go into melt-down. It didn't matter that few experts expected problems of this severity.*

Faber was referencing a *Vanity Fair* article (January 1999) laying out a doomsday scenario that was intended to either (take your pick) educate the masses or instill panic:

> *It is an instant past midnight, January 1, 2000. The power in some cities isn't working. Bank vaults and prison gates have swung open. Hospitals have shut down, so many countries degenerating into riots and revolution. No one will know the extent of its conse-quences until after they occur. The one sure thing is that the wondrous machines that govern and ease our lives won't know what to do.*

For some, it proved too good to be true and the opportunity of a life-time. In the words of Anthony Finkelstein, a software systems engi-neer at University College London, for many journalists at the time, the Y2K doomsday story was "simply too good to check." Y2K was the closest thing we had to a movie script about a race against time to fix the computers and save the world from annihilation, a classic illus-tration of Apocalyptic Awe, viewing dread as entertainment and allowing ourselves to be sucked into doomsday quicksand. But, for as astounding as it sounded, writer Lisa Fritscher asserted that the science behind the dilemma seemed sound:

The theory was that early computers were programmed to accept only two digits rather than four-digit dates. Meanwhile, 00 is not a recognized entry in binary computer language, leading to system failure in many cases. According to this theory, then, when the year rolled over from 99 to 00, the computers would crash.

Y2K did not bring about the destruction of civilization because the scientific community had anticipated the worst. Collectively, scientists, mathematicians, and computer programmers got the job done. Advanced computer systems easily accepted four-digit dates, while others were reprogrammed well in advance, preventing any kind of large-scale crash. Nevertheless, the Y2K aftershocks had been felt before in a never-ending cycle of AI fear.

Forced Labor

To go against God or to pretend to be like God is sure to evoke controversy. Karel Čapek was the Czech intellectual who coined the term "robot," derived from the Czech word *robota*, or forced labor. (Its Slavic linguistic root, *rab*, means "slave.") In his play *RUR*, (Rossum's Universal Robots), Čapek's fictitious inventor, Mr. Rossum, much like Victor Frankenstein, arrogantly attempts to prove that God is unnecessary. He wants to increase industrial production by creating artificial robots capable of performing the work of "two and a half men." John Jordon's book, *Robots,* reflected on these man-made slaves:

The contrast between robots as mechanical slaves and potentially rebellious destroyers of their human makers echoes Mary Shelley's "Frankenstein" and helps set the tone for later Western characterizations of robots as slaves straining against their lot, ready to burst out of control. The duality echoes throughout the 20th century: Terminator, HAL 9000, Blade Runner's replicants.

Following the 1921 premiere of *R.U.R.* Čapek warned of a dangerous future, telling the *London Saturday Review*:

The product of the human brain has escaped the control of human hands.

Three Laws of Robotics

Anticipating the potential loss of robotic control has been a meaningful topic within the science fiction community. Cathy Lowne and Patricia Bauer's *Britannica* article explored Isaac Asimov's *I, Robot* (1950), a collection of essays portraying robots programmed to think using ethical considerations—as opposed to mindless monsters running amuck:

> I, Robot, *was a collection of nine stories by science-fiction writer Isaac Asimov that imagines the development of "positronic" (humanlike, with a form of artificial intelligence) robots and wrestles with the moral implications of the technology.*

Asimov's "ethical programming" crafted a significant framework for science fiction, as summed up in his famed "Three Laws of Robotics":

1. A robot may not injure a human being or, through inaction, allow a human being to come to harm.
2. A robot must obey the orders given it by human beings except where such orders would conflict with the First Law.
3. A robot must protect its own existence as long as such protection does not conflict with the First and Second Laws.

Adhering to Asimov's "Three Laws" was the iconic Robby the Robot, first appearing in *Forbidden Planet* (1956) as a kind and humorous assistant. Although Robby was specifically programmed not to harm humans in any way, Asimov had warned of the dangers of robots revolting against humankind, an ongoing premise of early science fiction and the pulps.

HAL 9000

Mutinying AI represents the existential risk residing at the juncture where human promise becomes human horror, where our servants become our masters. For many, the illustration that immediately comes to mind is *2001: A Space Odyssey's* HAL 9000 (Heuristically programmed ALgorithmic computer), one of the most recognizable symbols of AI villainy in science fiction.

2001 was the invention of filmmaker Stanley Kubrick and sci-fi veteran Arthur C. Clarke, depicting astronauts investigating alien artefacts. The film shaped the public's perception of AI, inspiring filmmakers George Lucas, Steven Spielberg, and Christopher Nolan to reach for higher degrees of scientific accuracy, a departure from the childish special effects of the 1950s. With a glaring red eye and monotone voice, supercomputer Hal 9000 controlled the operations of a spacecraft on a mission to Jupiter. The unemotional, detached mechanism was aptly described by writer Celeste Neill:

> *The sentient computer's initial cold, logical demeanor which rapidly descends into murderous behavior has played a pivotal role in how AI has been perceived by the public in the last half-century of popular culture.*

HAL introduced us to the threat of dangerous technology, revisited in films such as *Alien (1979), Blade Runner (1982),* and *The Terminator (1984).* One of the initial offerings in this genre was *Westworld* (1973), portraying an amusement park catering to wealthy individuals willing to pay to live out their cowboy fantasies. Written and directed by Michael Crichton (1942–2008), who specialized in science fiction, techno-thrillers, and medical fiction in such works as *The Andromeda Strain* (1969), *Jurassic Park* (1990), and *Prey* (2002), *Westworld* was the first feature film to use 2D computer-digitized images to show the gunslinger's point of view. Crichton's plot involved a computer malfunction resulting in a rogue robot gunslinger (Yul Brynner) stalking the vacationers. *Westworld* helped construct the "bad robot" genre, that included the earlier HAL 9000, and triggered *Cosmos* writer Lauren Fuge to question how much autonomy should be granted to an AI:

> *HAL's rebellion in the film also touches on deeper ethical questions and predicts today's fear that AI could be used for sinister purposes.*

And, during these dark times, sinister purpose hangs in the air. Luigi Mangione was an Ivy League graduate and computer science major whose anti-capitalist views were inspired by "Unabomber" Ted Kaczynski. The Unabomber's anti-technology essays warned of a society breaking down by rapid changes in technology and the economy. Kaczynski argued that the expansion of industrial society was providing a false sense of freedom to individuals. Massive corporations could compromise our autonomy, pushing us to the point where we lose our self-sufficiency. The apocalyptic doom monger charged that:

> *Conservatives are fools: They whine about the decay of traditional values, yet they enthusiastically support technological progress and economic growth.*

Technology and corporate America have targets on their backs. After gunning down UnitedHealthcare CEO Brian Thompson, Mangione made amends, oddly writing, "These parasites had it coming. I do apologize for any strife and trauma, but it had to be done."

This may only be the beginning of more to come. With our improving capacity to predict the threat of hurricanes, tidal waves, and planet-destroying asteroids, heightened fears of the apocalypse have been unleashed, with disruptions in financial markets, critical infrastructure, and government institutions as primary concerns. The Y2K bug and HAL 9000 were merely harbingers of what might lie ahead, as observed by *The Washington Post*:

The emergence of AI has provoked great alarm in recent years, and for good reason. The technology could disrupt the economy, upending industries in unpredictable ways. Its awesome power deserves caution.

The "awesome power" of AI is no longer the domain of science fiction novels and pulp magazines but is now embedded into our daily lives, forcing us to rethink what we know. Isaac Asimov's "ethical programming," described in his "Three Laws of Robotics," was his altruistic wish that AI could be our faithful companions. But 75 years later, MIT researchers concluded they cannot make ethical decisions because they are unpredictable, highly "inconsistent and unstable," and "perhaps even fundamentally incapable of internalizing human-like preferences."

Fearing the worst, the 118-day strike of Hollywood actors, writers, and media professionals (2023) demanded that AI be kept in check and not used as a tool for exploitation. Like the Ancient Greek Laelaps, a mythological hound that always caught its prey, we need to look over our shoulders, because the hounds of AI have picked up our scent. Unlike HAL 9000, fear of AI is real, but—more importantly—our need for increased vigilance must be the first line of defense. Then president Bill Clinton organized efforts to minimize the anticipated Y2K disaster, calling the millennium bug "the first challenge of the 21st century successfully met." What Clinton didn't say, however, was that it won't be the last.

19

WHEN ROBOTS ATTACK

Technology, like an electronic pathogen, has metastasized, notably after the debut of CNN in 1980, an event that defined the new parameters of news journalism and the first 24-hour television news channel.

It grew larger, with white noise reverberating endlessly in global newsrooms and the realization that a hunger existed for this incessant drumbeat of doomscrolling and negative media coverage. And yes, most news coverage is negative and pessimistic, with a sliver of good news gratuitously placed at the end of the program. We are being bombarded with bad news and tragedy, the sounding of the trumpets draped in fear, and if that's not apocalyptical, then nothing is. But this is not Apocalyptic Awe, artfully transforming fear into fascination. No, this is commercial extortion, presenting "fear as fear itself," shamefully without pretense or excuse. It is the oldest trick in the book. We can't get away from it. And it keeps on coming.

AI's extensive reach has seeped into our daily lives. But where did this imaginative technology come from, and what makes it so powerful? Jerry Garcia's "long and strange trip" is an appropriate description, for AI has expanded. As detailed in the following chronology, there is nothing new under the sun. AI has been with us longer than you may think and is evolving faster than thought possible, and that's either good or not-so-good. The paranormal embodies the unknown—a dream state sensed before comprehended, felt before known. It slips through fingers like fog and is forgotten before our eyes are opened. Untangling the etherealism of the unknown is an impossibly daunting task, seducing us in a web of darkness and glowing light.

Like members of the *Titanic*'s string quartet, we stare into dark currents, fearing we will be swept out to a sea teeming with sea monsters and devoured by krakens and leviathans. The technological monster is like a thousand air-raid sirens screaming at the same time, shock waves exploding like electric popcorn. Everyone can feel the apprehension and the isolation; computer video screens, shiny plastic, and the AI voice of our choosing replace intimate human contact.

Circa 67 BC–205 BC: Discovered in 1901, the Antikythera mechanism has been hailed as an engineering marvel of ancient technology and the world's first analog computer. The device includes a sophisticated arrangement of gears and dials, a hand crank, interlocking gears, and multiple indicators that could show the date on both Egyptian and Greek calendars, track the positions of the sun, moon, and known planets within the zodiac, and even predict solar and lunar eclipses.

Circa 750–650 BC: Ancient Greek poets Hesiod and Homer were the first to describe robots. Hesiod described a giant bronze "living statue" built by Hephaestus, the Greek god of invention. Tom Curley, creator of *History Hogs*, said that although Talos' bronze composition and animated form shares similarities with robots, he is rooted in the realm of ancient mythology and divine craftsmanship:

Unlike contemporary robots, which are products of human engineering and technological advancement, Talos emerged from the creative hands of a god.

Talos was a giant, bronze automaton—a living statue forged by Hephaistos, the divine god of blacksmiths. But, according to some interpretations, Talos was not a creation of Hephaistos, but the last survivor of an ancient race of men fashioned from bronze.

Late 8th century BC: Homer's *Odyssey* includes a pair of robotic silver and gold watchdogs who guard over the palace of Alcinoos and who are described as possessing "intelligent minds."

1818: Mary Shelley's 19th-century gothic horror novel *Frankenstein* (1818) introduced the world to the concept of a scientist bringing a dead man to life, evolving into a masterpiece of horror and science fiction. According to Amanda Morgan, the public scorned *Frankenstein* because of the doctor "playing God" and creating life:

> *Dr. Frankenstein was able to create a life force, a concept critiqued by a more religious-centered society. At the time, this idea contradicted the idea that only God could create life. Creating a being through science was viewed as an abomination to human nature.*

1872: English author Samuel Butler published *Erewhcn,* which explored ideas of AI as influenced by Darwin's recently published *On the Origin of Species* (1859) and the Industrial Revolution's technological advances (e.g., mass steel production, the Watt steam engine, the cotton Gin, gas street lighting, the electromagnet, and the first photograph).

1912: On July 29, 1912, a bill was introduced to the Senate "to prohibit the making, showing, or distributing of fraudulent photographs." The law would make it illegal "to make, sell, publish, or show" any "fraudulent or untrue photograph, or picture purporting to be a photograph" of anyone who had not first given permission. Violation would see punishment of up to six months in jail or a fine up to $1,000 (~$31,800 adjusted for inflation).

1922: Czech playwright Karel Čapek wrote *R.U.R.* (Rossum's Universal Robots), describing a factory manufacturing artificial workers.

Čapek's concept aligned with Hephaestus, the ancient Greek god of the blacksmiths, who constructed automatons to help create other robots. After Čapek's American premier, the word *robot* entered the English-speaking lexicon—much like later terms, *flying saucer* (1947) and *bigfoot* (1958).

1941: German engineer Konrad Zuse constructed the Z3, the world's first programmable computer. The device was faster, more reliable, and better able to perform complicated calculations. Instructions were stored on an external tape, allowing it to function as a fully operational program-controlled system.

1946: ENIAC (Electronic Numerical Integrator and Computer), the first fully operational electronic general-purpose computer, was put into service at the University of Pennsylvania. Called a "giant brain" by the media, ENIAC weighed 30 tons and covered an area of about 1,800 square feet. The computer was made up of 40 individual panels configured in a U-shape.

1948: British mathematician and code-breaker Alan Turing mapped out the AI concept in a report titled *Intelligent Machinery.* What others called the "Turing Test" is still used today to measure a machine's ability to "think" like a human. Turing's research furthered public awareness of AI, especially after the release of the Oscar-nominated *The Imitation Game* (2014) and Turing's crucial work during World War II.

1950: Isaac Asimov was one of the first science fiction writers to explore AI's dark side, underscoring the necessity to create ethical guidelines to prevent harm to humans. His *I, Robot* series introduced the concept of the Three Laws of Robotics, which were meant to be irrevocable.

1956: Robby the Robot made his first cinematic appearance in MGM's *Forbidden Planet,* marking the first of 21 appearances throughout sci-fi history and into the 1960s and 1970s on television classics including *Lost in Space, Twilight Zone,* and *Mork & Mindy.* Robby is a kind and humorous assistant who is tasked with taking care of the Earthlings during their time on the planet. He is specifically programmed not to harm humans in any way.

1957: The successful Sputnik satellite launch set off a Cold War space exploration race between the Soviet Union and the U.S., as both sides began intensive research to discover technologies that would give them a military advantage.

1968: Stanley Kubrick's film 2001: A Space Odyssey introduced the supercomputer HAL 9000 into our national psyche, blending entertainment with apocalyptic warning of robots running amuck.

1969: The first AI robot, Shakey, had the ability to perform tasks that required planning, route-finding, and the rearranging of simple objects, and ability to perceive and reason about its surroundings. Shakey was referred to as the "first electronic person" (1970) by *Life* magazine and elected to the Carnegie Mellon's Robot Hall of Fame (2004.)

1997: A chess supercomputer called Deep Blue was built by the International Business Machines Corporation (IBM) and convincingly beat the reigning world champion, Garry Kasparov, in a six-game match. Deep Blue's 256 parallel processors enabled it to examine 200 million possible moves per second and to look ahead as many as 14 turns of play, marking the first time a computer won a match against a reigning world champion.

2004: The Defense Advanced Research Projects Agency (DARPA) challenged robotics enthusiasts to share intel and enter functioning self-driving cars into a desert-based competition.

2005: Stuxnet was a powerful computer worm (malware) believed to have been designed by U.S. and Israeli intelligence to disable a key part of the Iranian nuclear program. This cyberattack (coded Operation Olympic Games) was viewed as a nonviolent alternative to possible Israeli airstrikes against Iranian nuclear facilities

2007: The DARPA Urban Challenge invited entrants from Stanford, Carnegie Mellon, and other roboticists to enter self-driving cars in a city-environment competition, introducing lidar (laser imaging, detection, and ranging) and machine-learning-based artificial intelligence autonomous technologies.

2008: Before the advent of Fermilab's Large Hadron Collider, Tevatron, the most powerful particle accelerator in the United States, alarmed the scientific community who feared that the device would create black holes and "strangelets," simultaneously choking and collapsing the entire planet.

2009: Waymo, Google's secret and revolutionary self-driving vehicle project, was launched, introducing millions of riders to innovative precursor level 1–3 driver assist technologies.

2015. The *Falcon 9* successfully landed (through the guidance of computer vision being input into a route prediction algorithm).

2020: Amazon invested $1.2 billion in the self-driving startup Zoox, a robotaxi service that plans to transport customers in Las Vegas and San Francisco.

2023: For the first time in over six decades, strikes by the Screen Actors Guild, American Federation of Television and Radio Artists, and the Writers Guild of America demanded better pay and working conditions as they faced a landscape threatened by streaming and AI. Writing for *Harper's Bazaar*, Chelsey Sanchez underscored the problem areas:

> *The unregulated use of AI, which could be used to reproduce an actor's likeness or performance, has also been a point of contention at the bargaining table. SAG members were demanding guarantees as to how exactly AI will be deployed by studio and production companies.*

2023: The Hangzhou, China startup DeepSeek released an AI model called R1 on Apple and Google app stores. The chatbot showed advanced reasoning skills, such as the ability to rethink its approach to a math problem.

2023: The Beatles AI-assisted *Now and Then* was nominated for the Grammy Song of the Year. The song utilized AI to extract John Lennon's voice from an old demo, the same technology used to separate the Beatles' voices from background sounds during the making of director Peter Jackson's 2021 documentary series, *The Beatles: Get Back.*

2024: OFF Radio in Krakow, Poland replaced their journalists with virtual characters created by AI. But, after widespread outcries, the radio station ended its experiment with digital intelligence.

2023: Concerned with AI, the Recording Academy announced a series of changes to the Grammy Awards, including new protocols involving technological advancements, stating that, "Only human creators" could win the music industry's highest honor.

2024: Robert Downey Jr. threatened to sue Marvel executives—posthumously—if they ever recreate his portrayal of Tony Stark using AI. On the *On with Kara Swisher* podcast, the Oscar-winning actor said he intends to "sue all future executives" who allow an AI-created version of him. Downey said he did not want his Iron Man likeness to be recreated by AI technology:

2025: The apocalyptic Chicken Little, warning that the sky is falling, was Walt Disney's first fully computer-animated feature film, and the first film to be released in digital 3D.

2025: Co-authors of a MIT study investigating if AI devices can develop "value systems" concluded that they are unpredictable, highly "inconsistent and unstable," and perhaps even fundamentally incapable of internalizing human-like preferences.

2025: Disney and Universal sued Midjourney, the first time that major Hollywood companies have taken legal action against a maker of generative AI technology. The copyright lawsuit claimed the San Francisco-based company pirated from the two Hollywood studios to generate and distribute "endless unauthorized copies" of their famed characters, such as Darth Vader from the *Star Wars* franchise and the Minions from *Despicable Me*.

Our list doesn't end here. This is only the beginning of AI metastasizing in a mind-boggling multiplication of futuristic technology. There will be more to come, heading right at us, with warp speed.

20

THE CYBER DEEP STATE

Give me your tired, your poor,

Your huddled masses yearning to breathe free,

The wretched refuse of your teeming shore.

— EMMA LAZARUS

That warm sentiment from poet Emma Lazarus (1849–1887) is inscribed on the pedestal of the Statue of Liberty but could easily have been whispered inside the seductive rat-infested corridors of the internet. Of all the dark possibilities we have explored so far, the single-most concerning issue (to this researcher) is that of the Cyber Deep State. It is a foreboding place where the hearts of the disenfranchised are exploited and broken. For those without family, it becomes family. For those filled with anger, it provides targets. And for those without hope, it promises an anonymous community where the individual is encouraged to become a part of the conspiracy.

Tumbling down the conspiratorial rabbit hole, some slip from innocence to radicalism, seduced into a quagmire of disinformation.

Anonymous chat rooms use a "we against them" mantra that is repeated in an incessant drumbeat, gut-punching traditional values and established truths. The vulnerable are swayed by talk shows and chat rooms that incite anger at government and capitalistic institutions. As an example, Luigi Mangione, wearing a black, hooded windbreaker and mask, shot UnitedHealthcare CEO Brian Thompson three times and then escaped. Bullet casings left at the scene had the words "deny," "delay," and "depose" on them, an apparent reference to an insurance industry tactic for not paying claims. Mangione was arrested five days later and charged with the homicide. Investigators found a silencer, fake IDs, and a partially 3D-printed gun and bullets, along with a note to the FBI:

> To save you a lengthy investigation, I state plainly that I wasn't working with anyone.

Like the proverb of the pot calling the kettle "black," the Cyber Deep State incessantly rails against the "Deep State," waging war against amorphous government entities accused of implementing a New World Order. The Cyber Deep State is a dangerous Orwellian contagion, especially attractive to members of the tech savvy Generation Z, individuals such as Mangione, the 26-year-old suspect.

Thompson's death set off a series of cataclysmic (and, yes, that is the correct adjective) events that even Luigi Mangione could not have predicted. Recognized as one of America's largest corporations, UnitedHealth Group lost half its value—a shocking $288 billion—in the period of a month, its worst loss since the pandemic. In a humiliating public act, CEO Andrew Witty resigned after *The Wall Street Journal* revealed that UnitedHealth was under federal criminal investigation for possible Medicare fraud. *CNN's* Matt Egan followed the corporate unraveling:

> The trouble at UnitedHealth comes almost exactly six months after the murder of Brian Thompson, one of its top executives. The

brazen shooting of Thompson, in Midtown Manhattan, captured international attention and surfaced deep public resentment toward the healthcare industry

UnitedHealth is a member of the exclusive Dow Jones Industrial Average and is the nation's largest health insurer. Although Mangione played only a small role in its unfolding drama, his actions symbolized the resentment against capitalistic institutions propagated within the Cyber Deep State. But still, the question remains— what was the rabbit hole that he went down? Raised in privilege and affluence, and blessed with youthful good looks, Mangione was born with the proverbial silver spoon. But his privileged life did nothing to prevent him from being influenced by the anti-technology rantings of Ted Kaczynski, the so-called Unabomber. Described as a genius, madman, and murderer, Kaczynski was viewed by Mangione as an underground Robin Hood, an anti-hero resisting technology. As writer Clandis Time observed:

Naturally, Ted's antics drew the attention of the culture industry as soon as he was arrested. A flick through IMDb shows up a film from 1995, before he was even picked up by the FBI. Then we got the TV movie Unabomber: The True Story with Dean Stockwell, from Quantum Leap, The Story First: Behind the Unabomber, episodes of Time and Again, The FBI Files, 20/20, Undercover History, Aftermath with William Shatner—you get the idea.

Kaczynski, the most prolific serial bomber in U.S. history, orchestrated a 17-year bombing campaign. His 35,000-word *Industrial Society and Its Future* (1995) anti-technology treatise, commonly referred to as the *Unabomber Manifesto*, was published by *the New York Times*, *Washington Post*, and major newspapers. He called for a "revolution against the industrial system" that "may or may not make use of violence." He advocated for a return to "wild nature" unfettered by human management, interference, and control, writing that "freedom and technological progress are incompatible." He suggested that violence was an option. Writing for the *Deseret News*, Brooke Adams explored his rage:

> *In the manifesto, the Unabomber wrote that the Industrial Revolution and technological advances in society have been 'a disaster' for the human race. He blamed technology for destabilizing society, making life unfulfilling and causing widespread psychological suffering. Because of technological advances, most people spend their time engaged in useless, 'surrogate activities' pursuing artificial goals, such as scientific and technological work, consuming mass entertainment, following sports teams, etc.*

Like so many others, Mangione was "turned." In his review on *Goodreads*, he called Kaczynski a "political revolutionary," saying that "It's simply impossible to ignore how prescient many of his predictions about modern society turned out." Mangione quoted a description of Kaczynski he had seen online that noted Kaczynski "had the balls to recognize that peaceful protest has gotten us absolutely nowhere at the end of the day."

The far reach of the Cyber Deep State was evident in 2021, after hundreds of QAnon followers maxed out their credit cards, left their homes, and gathered on the grassy knoll in Dallas, Texas. It was 12:29, the exact time of day that President John F. Kennedy was shot 58 years earlier on November 22, 1963. These zealots, who believed that John F. Kennedy and John F. Kennedy Jr. would reappear in Dealey Plaza and reinstate Donald Trump as president, were influenced by cult leader Michael Brian Protzman. Calling himself "Negative 48," Protzman seemingly was at the right place at the right time. After Joe Biden defeated Trump in 2020, QAnon's mysterious "Q" stopped posting messages online, and Protzman stepped in to assume that role. Protzman's conspiracy theories attracted tens of thousands of followers.

Protzman, using his obsession with gematria, assigned numbers to letters of the alphabet for the word EVIL: E (5), V (22), I (9), L (12), totaling 48, and creating his online persona of "Negative 48." Protzman's fake gematria was based on a system he co-opted from a similar method developed by English occultist Aleister Crowley. According to *Vice* writer David Gilbert:

> *Protzman's popularity is built on a bastardized version of numerology known as gematria, a Jewish system of assigning a numerical value to a name, word, or phrase based on the letters used and inferring some sort of spiritual or mystical meaning behind the phrase.*

Protzman ranted online on a platform called Telegram (boasting more than one billion monthly active users as of March 2025) that the Kennedys were the descendants of Jesus Christ, and that JFK Jr. and JFK were coming back to help Trump purge the nation of a cabal of satanic pedophiles. *Rolling Stone* reporter Nikki McCann Ramirez observed that conspiratorial thinking has become a "default mechanism" for sowing distrust in the government deep state:

> *Protzman was a staple at Trump rallies, where the former president regularly makes thinly veiled callouts to QAnon's presence in his base. In the world of Q, no claim is too ridiculous, no theory too unfounded—so long as someone is willing to believe it.*

Protzman, who was born in the same year Kennedy was shot, was regarded as a godlike figure by his followers. Still, the failure of his predictions was not enough to dissuade his believers.

Humans are attracted to pseudoscience rather than to truth tethered to scientific fact. Many find science too restrictive and complicated. Like Linus waiting for the Great Pumpkin, 21st-century humans want their truths to be free, easy, and uncomplicated. Pseudoscience, brimming with illogical, free-flowing frivolity, is easier. It creates its own rules and moves the goalposts with ease. Complex topics can be comprehended in black and white terms, making the complexities of the world as easily understood as a *Roadrunner* cartoon.

As well, humans are a fickle lot, and the above simplistic explanation is sometimes flipped on its head. For example, many questioned the view that President John F. Kennedy's assignation resulted from Lee Harvey Oswald firing a fatal bullet into the back of his skull. A vocal majority refused to accept the single-bullet theory—only because it was too simplistic. They demanded sophisticated and complex answers. Conspiracy theorists were quick to offer that complexity in scattered theories that involved the CIA, the Mafia, Marilyn Monroe, the Soviet Union, and Cuba. The pickings were good. There was enough conspiracy on the vine for everyone.

There are numerous reasons why conspiracy theories provide a convenient get-out-of-jail-free card: (1) They require little cognitive ability. (2) They provide a modern-day role-play like *Dungeons and Dragons*. (3) They allow us to project our anger onto outside entities— the cabal, Israel, Biden, Trump, Venezuelan migrants, or alien beings. (4) During times of conflict (such as the COVID-19 pandemic or the drone hysteria of 2024), we can blame those we believe are withholding information. (5) It's more convenient to believe that an evil force is controlling our destiny than taking ownership of our lives.

What we know as "the truth" has been distorted as we question what is real. Conspiracy theories lie to us as they foreshadow what is to come. During the end times, the Tower of Babel and the voices of deception will be heard, the great wound of the world will bleed, and the mews of the dying beast will echo in our heads. Some believe that it's happening already.

Why did so many believe Alex Jones when he said that the 2012 school shooting at the Sandy Hook Elementary School didn't happen? Twenty first-graders and six educators were killed in Newtown, Connecticut, but Jones falsely called it a hoax. The conspiracy theorist also charged that Israel was responsible for the September 11 terror attacks that killed 2,977 people and that the

United Nations is engaged in a global depopulation program to create a "new world order."

During the internet's nascent dawn, the antigovernment movement (festering within what would become the Cyber Deep State) was finding a home. Alex Jones successfully channeled that anger into bombastic and hateful rants, promising to give voice to angry right-wing patriots and wage war against the New World Order. He spread his cancer, piggybacking on tragedies such as Waco, Oklahoma City, and Sandy Hook, as well as the ghost of Trans World Airlines Flight 800.

The First Internet Age Conspiracy

A new chapter of the anti-government playbook was created on July 17, 1996, after TWA flight 800 took off from Kennedy International Airport in the twilight of dusk. The 230 people aboard were on their way to Paris. The Boeing 747 jetliner leveled off at 13,700 feet and then, 12 minutes after takeoff, exploded. Thousands of pounds of kerosene were dumped from the plane's center as wing tanks ignited and vaporized. An orange fireball burned along the coastline as sections of the 747 plunged into the Atlantic Ocean.

Flight 800, regarded as the first Internet Age conspiracy, sparked a fierce debate among politicians, engineers, and conspiracy theorists. Some prominent examples included: (1) Pierre Salinger, former press secretary for Presidents Kennedy and Johnson, proclaimed that "friendly fire" from a Navy missile caused the crash. (2) Software engineer Michael E. Davis wrote a thesis titled, *Flight 800 Meteorite Interface Hypothesis—A Hypothetical Solution to the TWA Flight 800 Paradox*. (3) JK Henderson, a retired instrument engineer, suggested that a pressure issue may have caused the explosion. Five additional theories suggested: (1) The plane's front cargo door blew off. (2) Laser rays emitted from Long Island destroyed the aircraft. (3) Ball lightning caused the explosion. (4) A bolide exploded in Earth's atmosphere and sent one of its fragments into the plane's fuselage. (5) The missile theory.

The Missile Theory was like an uninvited guest that wouldn't go away. Conspiracy theorists alleged that a missile shot the jetliner down, and several mainstream media sources appeared to support those claims. *The Associated Press* proclaimed (June 19, 1996) that "Radar detected a blip merging with the jet shortly before the explosion, something that could indicate a missile hit." In another story (September 22, 1996), the *New York Post* reported:

> *Law enforcement sources said the hardest evidence gathered so far overwhelmingly suggests a surface-to-air missile.*

Because the public demanded more, the missile theory continued to resonate. A further *Associated Press* article, published on March 10, 1997, read:

> *The report said 'compelling testimony' indicated a missile hit the plane on the right side, forward of the wing, passing through the fuselage without exploding. This is consistent with a test missile with a dummy warhead*

Several books and documentaries followed. *TWA 800, the Crash, the Cover-Up, and the Conspiracy* (2016), written by investigative reporter Jack Cashill, concluded that the FBI, the CIA, and President Bill Clinton were involved in a cover-up. Although he had his share of supporters, Cashill was criticized for anti-government ranting about Benghazi and other right-wing themes with no connection to Flight 800. Some charged that the FBI misled the public after investigators identified 183 eyewitnesses who saw something rising from the ocean and strike Flight 800. They saw an explosion and the plane's wreckage dropping into the Atlantic Ocean. The FBI did not believe the eyewitnesses were accurate and disregarded their accounts. According to *MilitaryCorruption.com* writer David Smallwood:

A massive cover-up ensued, with the FBI suppressing the truth in an effort to save Bill Clinton's 1996 re-election chances. A surface-to-air missile that blasted the 747-100 right out of the sky, killing 230 people, becoming the third-deadliest aviation accident in U.S. history.

James Sander's book, *The Downing of TWA Flight 800* (1997), disclosed that he was given two samples of cloth from the seats. The fabric samples contained a bright red residue that had stained three rows of seats. After requesting that a non-government-linked laboratory test them, Sanders claimed that the first sample revealed elements consistent with the combustion byproducts of a military solid-fuel rocket motor of the powdered aluminum and perchlorate type. Airline veteran Andrew Danziger wrote an article for the *New York Daily News* titled *TWA Flight 800 was not blown up by a faulty fuel tank; it was shot down. I'll always believe that, and here's why.* He wrote:

Jets do not explode in midair. If they do, it's usually because they've been shot down or bombed. There's little to suggest that there was a bomb on board, but there is ample evidence that a missile of some sort detonated in the air very close to the plane and brought it down.

The tragedy prompted one of the most extensive aviation investigations in history. The NTSB eventually deemed it an accident and found no evidence of foul play. Former NTSB Board Member John Goglia, who spent four years investigating the crash, addressed The TWA 800 Project, a group of petitioners who wanted the NTBS to reopen the crash investigation, claiming that a "detonation or high-velocity explosion" caused the crash. Goglia wrote in *Forbes* (July 2014) that eyewitness accounts of a "flash" in the sky just before the airplane blew up were not supported by radar evidence. The fuselage wreckage also did not show any evidence of an explosion next to the plane, he concluded:

> At the end of the day, 'damage patterns within the airplane were
> consistent with a center wing tank explosion.' In addition, the debris
> pattern was consistent with a fuel-air explosion in the center wing
> tank. The NTSB concluded that the petitioners had not introduced
> any evidence which would warrant overturning the Board's prior
> conclusions or determination of probable cause.

Investigators concluded the streak observed by hundreds of witnesses
was burning fuel streaming from the plane's wing tank—part of the
95% of the aircraft that was recovered. A 93-foot segment of the
aircraft fuselage was reconstructed and moved to a 30,000 square foot
hangar in Ashburn, Virginia. The reconstructed plane was used in
accident investigation training for nearly 20 years and decommis-
sioned in July 2021. The remains of all passengers were recovered,
and all 230 names were etched into the TWA Flight 800 International
Memorial at Smith Point County Park on Long Island.

The Boeing had 18 crew members, including four pilots and 14 flight
attendants. There was no documentation of the flight crew reporting
a problem to air traffic control, and while officials believe they have
found the answer, over 20 years later, we will never know conclusively
what really happened. The NTSB's official report, issued four years
after the crash, concluded an electrical spark ignited fuel vapors in
the center fuel tank and was the probable cause of the explosion.
This finding led to regulations requiring a system that pumps inert
gas into empty fuel tanks. Boeing was required to replace the brittle
wiring on other 747s and redesign their air conditioning packs.

The Flight 800 crash was the first conspiracy theory to emerge on the
budding World Wide Web's Cyber Deep State. At that time,
"Unabomber" Ted Kaczynski (who had never seen Facebook or sent
or received an e-mail) was living in a remote cabin in Montana
without electricity or running water and writing his anti-technology
protests. Flight 800 proved to be ground zero for conspiracy theorists,
who, like flies drawn to stink, immediately began spreading misinformation, as documented by *USA Today's* David M. Zimmer:

One early version posted online alleged the crash resulted from an attack designed to kill former U.S. Secretary of State Henry Kissinger, who was, in fact, not on board. Another claimed the friendly fire was intended to kill former Arkansas state troopers once assigned to then-President Bill Clinton's security detail.

Still, once again, we need to ask, why do individuals accede to unhinged conspiracies devoid of any factual basis? Millions of followers have embraced hate mongers such as Alex Jones, who has turned truth into mush through his inflammatory rhetoric and website, as noted by Candice Jeffries:

Via both his radio show and news site, Jones has used tragic American events like the Sandy Hook shooting, the Oklahoma City bombing, the terrorist attacks on Sept. 11, 2001, the bombings at the Boston Marathon, and the recent shootings in Las Vegas to sprout controversial theories about our government. As the Southern Poverty Law Center's website puts it, "Time after time, he warns without any evidence that terrorist attacks... are actually 'false flag' operations by our government or evil 'globalist' forces planning to take over the world.

The fearmonger did have his day in court. Jones admitted in 2022 that the Sandy Hook shooting was "100 percent real" and that it was "absolutely irresponsible" to call it a hoax. He was ordered to liquidate his personal assets after relatives of the victims won a defamation lawsuit of more than $1.5 billion. Reporter Sarah Rumph called Jones "a rotten-to-the-core spewer of rancid bovine excrement," while the Southern Poverty Law Center called him "one of the most prolific and influential conspiracy theorists in contemporary America":

Jones' most notable conspiracies revolve around national tragedies and terrorist attacks he labels as 'false flag' operations. With millions of regular viewers and over two decades on the air, Jones

*has created a financial and brand empire out of selling misinforma-
tion and disinformation, as well as self-help dietary products.*

*His uncorroborated reporting has led to many innocent people being
harassed by internet trolls both online and in person. His politically
charged stunts have made headlines, and by 2021, his calls for
Trump supporters to protest the Biden presidency helped fuel the
Jan. 6 insurrection on the U.S. Capitol building.*

There is truth and there are lies, and one must be wise enough to
separate the two. We are looking for answers, yes, but must be vigi-
lant because, even now, we are under attack from false prophets on
the left and right, from the front and rear. We are mere infants suck-
ling on spoon-fed pablum provided by the Cyber Deep State.

Still, in the hope of completing this circle, we need to ask, what harm
do individuals like Alex Jones do to a society based on the merits of
free speech when his speech is filled with hatred and lies? And what
responsibility should individuals like Jones take, when his rants are
akin to someone shouting "fire" in a crowded theatre? Although
Jones had no role in the TWA Flight 800—it was before his time—he
was able to exploit the death, anger, and rage of similar events, effectively poisoning vulnerable minds.

The laws of the universe are random, scattered, and non-linier,
composed of incongruous and novel outliers—bad things happen to
good people, justice doesn't always prevail, and sometimes the bad
guys win. We can't always make sense of the universe, because, like
the paranormal, it is murky at best. It's easier to believe in conspiracy
theories than to accept that, often, there is no rhyme or reason for the
way the universe unfolds in our time of fear and hour of need.

21

THE DRONE HYSTERIA OF 2024

P rotection and security, the government's most important responsibilities, are crucial for citizens to feel safe and reassured. This principle was put into play after America entered World War II, with President Franklin Delano Roosevelt's rallying cry, "We have nothing to fear but fear itself." Yet, 83 years later, during the drone hysteria of 2024, the American people were left feeling let down by the government and a pervasive conspiracy that eroded confidence and sowed doubt.

After Halloween

Appropriately, it all started a few weeks after Halloween. New Jersey reporter Amanda Wallace wrote that, on Tuesday, November 18, 2024, patrol officers had observed drone activity. Wallace said that the frenzy began to gain traction on social media:

> Over the past few weeks, New Jersey residents have been reporting alleged sightings of large, mysterious drones hovering in the night sky. The sightings, which began in the week before Thanksgiving, have since been reported to law enforcement from several North

Jersey counties. Photos, videos and reported sightings of the suspected drones have been flooding social media, even leading to the creation of Facebook groups dedicated to solving the mystery.

And the mystery only grew. The drones, some the size of small cars, were described as operating near military installations and critical infrastructure, including the Verrazzano-Narrows Bridge. New York Governor Kathy Hochul confirmed that drone activity shut down runways at Stewart International Airport, located about 60 miles north of New York City. Hochul asked federal authorities to authorize local police departments to shoot them down. As anxiety heightened, internet pathogens took advantage of the situation. A contrived video, piecing together Department of Defense clips and ominous music, circulated over the internet. The video, drawing over nine million viewers, implied that the drones were extraterrestrial:

A number of mysterious drones have been reported flying over New Jersey and other parts of the eastern U.S., fueling speculation about their origin. The Pentagon has confirmed that the mysterious drones appearing worldwide are not of earthly origin. They are not U.S. Military drones, and they are not foreign entities or adversaries.

That Department of Defense hoax went unchallenged. Secretary of Homeland Security Alejandro Majorkas was unable to explain the drone anomaly coherently. John Kirby, the spokesperson for the National Security Council, was unconvincing when he said that the government had not identified anything anomalous and "did not assess the activity to present a national security risk." Still, it took an unprecedented joint statement from the Department of Homeland Security, the FBI, the Federal Aviation Administration, and the Department of Defense to explain:

Having closely examined the technical data and tips from concerned citizens, we assess that the sightings to date include a combination of lawful commercial drones, hobbyist drones, and law enforcement drones, as well as manned fixed-wing aircraft, helicopters, and stars mistakenly reported as drones.

Conspiracy theories dwell in an atmosphere of ignorance. President-elect Donald Trump contributed to the chaos by saying that the government knows what the drones are and where they came from. "Our military knows, and our president knows, and for some reason, they want to keep people in suspense."

John Ferguson, chief executive of drone manufacturer Saxon Aerospace, insisted he was not trying to spread "misinformation or scare people," but said that a missing Soviet-era nuclear warhead had been transported from Ukraine to the U.S. Ferguson explained there was "no reason for drones to be in the air at night unless you're doing some type of ISR work—intelligence, surveillance, reconnaissance." His TikTok video propelled the story that government drones were looking for a nuclear device. It racked up more than 15 million views on X. It was all-hands-on deck. Former Department of Defense official, and high-profile whistleblower, Luis Elizondo conjectured that military drones could possibly be searching for these weapons:

> *Maybe some rogue nation was able to put something really bad here, some sort of Weapons of Mass Destruction here in the continental United States, maybe we don't want to scare the public. So, what do we do? We put out these drones with sniffers and try to find something maybe that's hopefully not there. Is that a possibility? Sure.*

Pareidolia

So, what exactly did they see? During the September 11, 2001 attacks, television viewers allegedly saw the face of Satan in clouds of smoke rising from the World Trade Center. Mark D. Philips, the photojournalist who captured what appeared to be an ominous face in the smoke, questioned what his photo really showed:

> Is it just "light and smoke" as the pundits say, or is it the "face of pure evil" as the public believes?

Experts say this was an example of pareidolia, a type of apophenia or patternicity characterized by seeing or hearing patterns or images in random events, either visual or auditory, where one doesn't exist. Apophenia isn't uncommon, and pareidolia is often mentioned within the Bigfoot community, citing "witnesses" who have misinterpreted stimulus, so that one sees an object, pattern, or Bigfoot where there is none. Pareidolia includes hearing voices in random noise or stillness. Astrophysicist Carl Sagan believed that hallucinations, ranging from hearing voices to seeing shapes when no one is present, are common experiences brought about by factors, including sensory deprivation, sleep disturbances, high fever, migraines, and the use of certain drugs. Hallucinations have often been interpreted as supernatural experiences, and many indigenous cultures have rituals and practices centered around their interpretation.

Four Questions

Even so, the 2024 drone mystery demanded answers: (1) Could the New Jersey drones have been an example of pareidolia? (2) Could social and media frenzy have contributed to a form of mass hallucination shared by thousands? (3) Do humans have an innate need to confabulate, fill in the blanks, and create homeostasis? (4) Have we experienced anything like this before? Those are good question with too few answers. Writer Jacob Weindling observed that "people were seeing anomalous things in the sky that very clearly were not planes or constellations." He said:

> It's easy to just dismiss this as all a hallucination of a clearly traumatized populace currently silently and not so silently cheering for

murder, but the statements on the record from authorities don't reflect that. 'We're just waiting for our federal partners to let us know what's going on' and the Department of Defense saying on December 17th that the 'FBI has received tips of more than 5,000 reported drone sightings in the last few weeks with approximately 100 leads generated' do not suggest that this is all just an invention of people's imaginations.

The drone hysteria was reminiscent of Orson Welle's 1938 radio drama of H.G. Wells' *The War of the Worlds*—adapting the 40-year-old novel into fake news bulletins describing a Martian invasion of Grover's Mill, New Jersey. A. Brad Schwartz, author of *Broadcast Hysteria: Orson Welles' War of the Worlds and the Art of Fake News* (2016), investigated the newspaper sensationalism and hysteria surrounding the broadcast:

Some listeners mistook those bulletins for the real thing, and their anxious phone calls to police, newspaper offices, and radio stations convinced many journalists that the show had caused nationwide hysteria. By the next morning, the 23-year-old Welles's face and name were on the front pages of newspapers coast-to-coast, along with headlines about the mass panic his CBS broadcast had allegedly inspired.

People were angry, and Welles was confronted with reports of mass stampedes, suicides, and angered listeners threatening to shoot him on sight. The director had to answer "dozens of reporters, photographers, and newsreel cameramen at a hastily arranged press conference" asking why he panicked his audience. Another example of societal apprehension arose after the 2023 Chinese spy balloons that caused, not only unnecessary public anxiety, but a lack of clarification from a government some felt was not being transparent enough.

Craft from Outer Space

The *War of the World*'s theme was repeated by Representative Nancy Mace (R-SC), warning that the federal government was lying to the American people. She said the drones may be "craft from outer space." Interviewed on the podcast *Outkicks*, Mace admitted that she participated in UAP hearings and revealed "there are some that are unexplained" and "the odds are in your favor" that extraterrestrial life exists in the universe. Chad Wilson, in his article *Decoding the Drone Phenomenon Alien Craft or Human Tech?* wrote:

> *Some UFO enthusiasts propose that these events might indicate a systematic effort by an extraterrestrial intelligence to study Earth's surface, its population, or its infrastructure. The grid-like flight patterns and apparent focus on rural areas might suggest an intent to avoid heavily populated regions while conducting precise surveys or collecting data.*

Everyone was trawling through uncharted seas with nothing to guide them but opinion, while Wilson quipped, "I wish the aliens would hurry up and invade already," quipped pop culture authority Stephen Johnson, writing in *Life Hacker*:

> *No one wants it to be aliens more than me. Even if they're planning to force us to work in outer space diamond mines, I'd still welcome alien overlords. But it's never aliens. The 'drones' everyone is seeing are not aliens. They aren't foreign invaders, or part of a secret government project, or anything else cool either. No one can say with 100% certainty, but I'd bet my collection of solid gold backscratchers that the recent wave of reports of unidentified flying objects is because people are very bad at identifying objects.*

Have we witnessed this before? After Kenneth Arnold's sighting on June 24, 1947, a "Flying Saucer" wave was upon us and everyone who was looking at the skies saw something. But, according to a Gallop

Poll, less than 1% of the population believed they were extraterrestrial in origin; 16% attributed them to an American or Russian secret weapon.

Rorschach Inkblot

Missy Cummings, an engineering professor at George Mason University who has studied drones for 25 years, told CBS what most people thought were drones were actually aircraft, stars, or reflections off objects, like towers:

> *Of all of those options, drones are the least likely, because it's actually pretty hard to pick these out of the sky. If you're actually looking at lights from a drone, it means you're definitely not looking at a foreign adversary, because they're sophisticated enough to turn the lights off.*

Robert E. Bartholomew believes that individuals tend to project their fears onto ambiguous stimuli. As a result, the sky becomes a Rorschach inkblot test where people often see what they expect to see:

> *To my eyes, this is another classic case of patternicity: the tendency to see meaningful patterns in meaningful and meaningless noise. Here the fact that photographs and videos of the objects are almost all taken at night, are grainy and blurry, makes the phenomena ripe for people filling in whatever their imagination conjures.*

Bartholomew's article, *The Great Drone Panic of 2024... and 1914* looked at social and political unrest, such as those surrounding tensions between the United States and Russia and geopolitical conflicts in the Middle East that can lead to misinterpreting of anomalies like the New Jersey drones:

One of the more far-fetched explanations for the current scare is that a Chinese or Iranian vessel is stationed off the east coast and is launching the drones to spy on our military bases or even launch a terrorist attack with explosives.

Societal panics, even decades apart, share common ground. What were once thought to be German and Japanese espionage devices are now believed to belong to China or Iran. The same mass anxiety surrounding mysterious lights in the skies have prompted people to look up and search for images that don't actually exist (pareidolia).

Typically, UFO/UAP sightings are explained away as government stealth technology obtained through an adversary or anonymously. New Jersey state senator Jon Bramnick accused the federal government of hiding the truth and called for officials to declare a limited state of emergency and close the airspace. He told *NewsNation* the government "doesn't want us to know" because it was "fearful" of how the public would react:

If they're saying it's not a threat it must be something going on that's real, real top secret... What that must mean is they're more concerned with us getting knowledge and being afraid of that information than having no knowledge and having all these questions.

Pummeled by a hurricane of innuendo, the truth was compromised by a relentless number of variables reeking of uncertainty. (1) The Biden Administration was unable to provide a clear message about what the drones were. (2) President-elect Donald Trump stated that the government was involved in a conspiracy of silence. (3) Representative Nancy Mace suggested that the drones may be "craft from outer space." (4) An internet video falsely claimed that the Department of Defense said the drones were "not from this planet." (5) Drone manufacturer John Ferguson said that terrorists may have stolen a nuclear warhead from Ukraine. (6) New Jersey senator Jon Bramnick called for a state of emergency. (7) The FAA limited drone flights over New Jersey's power stations and infrastructure.

The lack of convincing explanations about what was flying over the New Jersey skies sparked an escalating national mania, revisited in restaurants, taverns, and family dining rooms. Social media fanned the flames. Hysteria hovered in the air. And, like little children, we looked fearfully at the skies just like we did back in 1938, awaiting a possible flying saucer invasion and bug-eyed men from Mars.

22

FEARMONGERING IN THE HERE
AND NOW

After its brazen 2025 attack on Russian air bases thousands of miles from the Ukraine border, Russian hardliners called for Ukraine's nuclear obliteration, issuing threats of Armageddon. According to CNN's Matthew Chance:

> *The Kremlin's recently updated nuclear doctrine – which sets out conditions for a launch – states that any attack on 'critically important' military infrastructure which 'disrupts response actions by nuclear forces' could trigger a nuclear retaliation.*

Russia has the world's largest nuclear arsenal and, together with the U.S.' controls 88% of the world's nuclear warheads. In 2024, Kremlin chief Vladimir Putin changed Russia's official nuclear doctrine, warning the West that Russia could use nuclear weapons if it or ally Belarus were struck with conventional missiles, and that Moscow would consider any assault on it supported by a nuclear power to be a joint attack:

> *It is proposed that aggression against Russia by any non-nuclear*

state, but with the participation or support of a nuclear state, be considered as their joint attack on the Russian Federation.

While Russia warns that NATO is risking a global war, Ukraine accuses Putin of "nuclear blackmail." That rhetoric is being backed up with a mighty fist. Russia's invasion of Ukraine on February 24, 2022, triggered the gravest confrontation between Russia and the West since the 1962 Cuban Missile Crisis, the closest the two super-powers came to nuclear war. And, although this is a well-worn example of Kremlin saber rattling, keep in mind that a nuclear launch may be as elemental as three individuals, deep inside Siberian doomsday bunkers, turning their keys at the same time. Three men. Three keys. One mushroom cloud.

Beginning with the Great Flood stories of Noah, the Black Plague, threats of the Cold War, global warming, nuclear winters, and total annelation, end-of-the-world scenarios have been scrawled across the torn pages of history. Uncertainty surrounding ancient Revelation texts and the ticking of the modern-day Doomsday Clock suggest that Armageddon is right on schedule.

Fear rules. It is the mother of emotions and the ultimate deal-breaker. For an example, just look at the 2024 election results that seem to have occurred a million years ago. It wasn't that long ago, but no matter; everyone got it wrong—pundits and voters alike—viewing it through tinted funhouse glasses, making objects appear distorted, closer, or farther than they were. The 2024 election wasn't about the economy, illegal immigration, reproductive and transgendered rights, or preserving democracy. Yes, those platforms were the issues voters most frequently discussed, but they were only dog whistles and fire alarms that stoked our emotions and raised our hackles.

The 2024 election wasn't an attempt at commonsense problem-solving and choosing the worthiest candidate. No, something else was in play—not cognitively, not something that begged for rational thought, but something resonating on a base, reptilian level; a gorilla-like chimera that picked us up, shook us, and threw us to the ground.

- The 2024 election focused on two opposing philosophical platforms. Kamala Harris' message of joy and optimism versus Donald Trump's message of fear. The talking points were clear. You could not miss them. Harris straddled the divide between supporting Israel and supporting Arab Americans devastated over Gaza. She attempted to give voice to all sides. She was the first woman of color at the top of a major-party ticket. She broke fundraising records, raising $1 billion in less than three months. Celebrity endorsements ranged from pop star Taylor Swift to former California governor Arnold Schwarzenegger.

Harris was concerned with climate change. Trump called it a hoax.

But Trump also had weapons lined up—personalities like Hulk Hogan, Elon Musk, and Robert F. Kennedy Jr.—and watched as his war chest overflowed. More importantly, Trump effectively rang the bell of doom, warning against: (1) Illegal aliens. (2) Haitians eating cats and dogs. (3) Mexican drug cartels. (4) Fentanyl across the border. (5) Israel-Iran at war. (7) Russia-Ukraine War. (8) Forced sex change operations on our children. (9) The Washington, D.C. swamp.

One Trump supporter, in a letter to the editor, offered his personal laundry list of complaints: (1) The destructive riots of 2020 were called peaceful by the media. (2) The deification of the drug thug George Floyd. (3) The forced acceptance of transgenderism in children as a normal part of self-identification. (4) The failure of Democrat-run cities to control criminal elements in the name of equity. (5) The government programmed over-running of our borders. (6) The unrealistic mandate to produce electric vehicles.

Those lies and distortions of the truth were a carpet-bombing campaign that came and went. Some resonated while others slipped away, unchallenged. Potential voters were being assaulted, beaten, and worn down. There were other issues, some deeply embedded inside the walls of conspiracy theory, but attracting swells of believers and a fierce advocate. Trump was the counterpuncher, the junkyard dog with the teeth to rip out the heart of liberalism and retake our cities, as he championed right-wing extremism. He was the "outsider" who was going to drain the swamp. He was bombastic, crude, and impossible to ignore. He constantly reminded us that the end of our democracy was near, that our economy would collapse, and that we were on the brink of World War III. Trump played his deck of fear cards—again and again. And it wore us down.

Voters had a choice, and after the votes were counted, it became apparent that the attraction to joy was not as powerful as the avoidance of fear. Fear and lies worked better than truth and joy. Throughout the presidential campaign, President-elect Donald Trump was both a subject and spreader of numerous falsehoods. *USA Today* reporter Chris Mueller noted that:

> *Trump has made false claims too, including his oft-repeated assertion that he lost to Joe Biden in 2020 due to election fraud. He also falsely claimed that millions of noncitizens vote in U.S. elections, that Haitian migrants in Ohio ate pets and that the government didn't have money to help hurricane victims because it was spent on migrants living in the country illegally.*

If a lie is repeated enough times, people will believe it. Nazi propaganda chief Joseph Goebbels is believed to have made that statement; it defines Trump's "big lie" and the danger of totalitarianism. Goebbels said:

> *If you tell a lie big enough and keep repeating it, people will eventually come to believe it. The lie can be maintained only for such time as the State can shield the people from the political, economic, and/or military consequences of the lie. It thus becomes vitally*

important for the State to use all of its powers to repress dissent, for the truth is the mortal enemy of the lie, and thus by extension, the truth is the greatest enemy of the State.

The disinformation continued. Speaking to attendees at the World Economic Forum in Davos, Trump boasted that he won by millions of votes in the 2024 election, which gave him "a massive mandate from the American people, like hasn't been seen in many years." That was false. Trump knew it, and so did the AP's Melissa Goldin:

Trump's margin of victory in the 2024 election was not as large as he makes it seem. He won the electoral vote 312 to 226, including all seven swing states. The popular vote, however, was far closer, with Trump receiving 49.9% of the vote with 77,303,573 votes cast to Harris' 75,019,257 votes (48.4%), according to AP Vote Cast. That's a difference of 2,284,316 votes. In 2020, Joe Biden defeated Trump by more than 7 million votes.

Futurist George Orwell was correct, and so was H.P. Lovecraft, who foretold of a "new dark age." Maranda Gurzo established that Lovecraft was able to predict with some precision the crisis of Western civilization, which we are witnessing. As Lovecraft wrote:

[A crisis that] even before being environmental, economic, political and social, is a crisis of founding values and meaning and whose effects we can evaluate by noting the ever-growing nihilism that seems to erode modern civilization at all levels, now founded only on finance and materialism which often, though not always, translates into a consumerism led to excess.

Lovecraft's prophesies have stood the test of time and attracted an audience marching to his pessimism drumbeat. Some believe the end is near as they count the remaining days. Since the election results of 2024, books espousing dark futuristic narratives and dystopian worlds have been among Amazon's best sellers. *The Handmaid's Tale*

(1985), Margaret Atwood's dystopian classic about a country in which women are brutally repressed, has been high on the list, as well as George Orwell's *Nineteen Eighty-Four* (1949) and Ray Bradbury's *Fahrenheit 451* (1953). Other films, like *I Am Legend* (2007) and *Children of Men* (2010), depict dire futures and the struggle for survival. The warning signs are numerous. The crisis Lovecraft prophesized would unfold "when the stars are right," an apocalyptic nightmare revealed in *Dagon* (1917), his first story:

> *The day when they come out of the waves and clasp in immense claws the remains of insignificant humanity worn out by wars... the day the lands will sink and the dark bottom of the oceans will rise to the surface, in universal pandemonium.*

There were other creative minds that helped us understand the understandable and keep things in perspective. Pete Seeger's *Turn, Turn, Turn"* (1962) spoke of "a time to kill, a time to heal. A time to laugh, a time to weep." But in between Seeger's lines were images of those weeping in fear of death. Fear is the monster in the room. It's always there and it wins every time.

Just look at the 2,284,316 people who cast votes in 2024, and then think about what drove them to vote as they did.

23

THE PRIMAL BEAST

Therefore, do not be anxious about tomorrow, for tomorrow will be anxious for itself. Sufficient for the day is its own trouble.

— MATTHEW 6:34

One of humankind's most primitive responses is the gut connection. The gut response is when we get slammed in the belly by the demons of impending doom, what Joshua Hicks of Texas A&M's Department of Psychological and Brain Sciences called "Just knowing without knowing how or why." It's the same for us as it is for a rat being stared down by a snake. We don't have time to think about it. It just happens—the belly knows what it knows. It responds before the brain can assimilate the stimuli and process it and make sense of it. The belly communicates on a primal, reptilian level; it is more powerful than our cognitive abilities. And more immediate.

The Belly Knows What It Knows

Consider the dynamics of this reptilian emotion that hijacks our soul, dragging us into a dark unforgiving pit. Fear is a primary survival mechanism. After a perceived threat, it triggers a visceral response creating an adrenaline explosion of rapid heartbeat, elevated body temperature, sweat, and terror.

Whenever we feel threatened, fear prepares us for action. Our bodies release hormones that ramp up or slow down natural functions. For example, our digestive system shuts down during any physical or psychological attack as our heart rate quickens. As a result, more blood flows to the muscles, and eyesight is enhanced. We are ready for fight or flight.

The faces of fear don't always emanate from dark alleyways and stairwells, but can be embedded within the scar tissues of our inner psyche, where the trolls of suspicion and apprehension dwell. Some individuals are prisoners of the past. They are shackled to childhood nightmares that strangle them in adulthood. What child has not been lectured about their wickedness and what their punishment will be? They feel ashamed to admit that they are afraid, because fear is often regarded as "childish."

We dance out of fear and madness and with synchronized footsteps of confusion. A phobia, an abnormal degree of fear, can involve persistent anxiety, as evidenced by individuals who count each second before the monster's next attack. Sometimes what is said is less important than subtle nuances and implications. Perceived feelings of social pain, like rejection and loneliness, activate the same neural pathways as fear. Sometimes, a mere suggestion can provoke an unpleasant response. It can start as just a nanogram—a ripple in the ocean, as additional ripples turn the tide into a tsunami, resulting in a crippling paralysis of excessive fear. The North American Nursing Diagnosis Association (NANDA) offers a definition, calling excessive fear:

> *[...] an intense and disproportionate emotional state that arises in response to a perceived imminent threat, leading to a range of physiological and psychological reactions that are often overwhelming*

and debilitating. Individuals experiencing excessive fear may exhibit a heightened state of alertness, marked by symptoms such as nervousness, tension, and psychomotor agitation, which can disrupt their ability to concentrate and control impulses.

NANDA says the phobia can diminish an individual's self-confidence and ability to cope, leading to avoidance behaviors and a persistent focus on the source of their fear. A similar condition is post-traumatic stress disorder (PTSD), a phobia caused by an overwhelmingly trauma. PTSD renders the victim in a constant state of hyper-alertness, steeling themselves for the next explosion, sexual assault, or traumatic event. Traumatized individuals tend to retraumatize themselves. Sleepwalking in a mechanical trance, as a moth drawn to a flame, they revisit the event. And like an unholy experiment of Dr. Moreau, it transforms the individual into a helpless, medicated zombie, a lost soul pitied by family and hated by self.

Wrapped in fear and anxiety, these individuals may suffer from additional phobias that include agoraphobia (the fear of open or crowded spaces), claustrophobia (the fear of small, enclosed spaces), and monophobia (the fear of being alone). Harvard University's Center for the Developing Child believes that a fear-based environment disrupts brain development. If left untreated, the trauma becomes even more damaging:

Science shows that exposure to circumstances that produce persistent fear, and chronic anxiety can have lifelong consequences by disrupting the developing architecture of the brain. These experiences cause changes in brain activity and have been shown to have adverse long-term implications for learning, behavior, and health.

Fight, flight, or freeze are tactics used by all animals, but a fourth tactic—belonging—is far stronger and goes beyond physical survival. Maslow's Hierarchy of Needs denotes that belonging is a powerful drive that prompts us to join a group for love and connection. There is strength and safety in numbers and in developing a non-confrontational groupthink. That need to belong is the driving force that motivates individuals to have intimate relationships with family and friends, and, for some, to join gangs and cults.

Apocalyptic Awe, vicariously experiencing doomsday horror through motion pictures, music, and literature, helps put them in a controlled space. Psychologists use a number of techniques to control fear, including exposure therapy, where individuals gradually face their fears in a controlled environment. The process of desensitization, a measured exposure to the feared object or situation, helps to reduce sensitivity over time, giving the fear shape and parameters.

Remarkably, examples of Apocalyptic Awe are not difficult to find. The 1977 motion picture *The End of the World* left nothing to the imagination, while *Doomsday* (2008) looked at the aftermath of a deadly virus outbreak. "We interrupt our regular programming to bring you this Special Bulletin from RBS News" was the introduction to the television film *Special Bulletin* (1983), about a terrorist group attempting to blackmail the U.S. government into disabling its nuclear weapons. It simulates a series of live news broadcasts on the fictional RBS Network, similar to Orson Welle's 1938 *The War of the Worlds* radio drama.

When the Primal Beast Is Not Contained

In Buddhist teachings, there is a difference between healthy fear and unhealthy fear. Healthy fear is a normal response to something that can harm us; for example, walking away from the edge of a deep ravine or choosing not to smoke for fear of lung cancer. This healthy fear can keep us safe and ultimately save our lives. It motivates us to avoid danger.

Unhealthy fear is when we fear things that cannot harm us (and, yes, we can debate this), ordinary objects like spiders, clowns, and the apocalypse. Unhealthy fear can include fear of rejection or failure.

Individuals who endure prolonged periods of fear, from physical dangers or perceived threats, breathe life into this monster even as it drains their psychic energy. On this topic, Dr. Charles Stanley, founder and president of In Touch Ministries, wrote:

> Fear stifles our thinking and actions. It creates indecisiveness that results in stagnation. I have known talented people who procrastinate indefinitely rather than risk failure. Lost opportunities cause erosion of confidence, and the downward spiral begins.

We cannot live in a world without fear, but we have the ability to harness those toxic voices. Gautama Buddha (c. 483 BCE or 400 BCE) called these fears "delusions" because they were distorted ways of viewing the world. He said:

> If we learn to control our mind and reduce and eventually eliminate these delusions, the source of all our fear, healthy and unhealthy, is eradicated.

Unhealthy fear kills the spirit and numbs the soul and, if not eradicated, will doom all future optimism. It keeps us mired in a quicksand that strips away our extraordinary potential, as motivational writer Iain Legg believes:

> Many of us shy away from risk because we fear negative consequences. For example, you may hesitate to invest your money because you fear losing it or avoid starting a new relationship because you were so hurt by the last one. What most of us fail to realize is that risk can also bring great rewards. Avoiding risk may help us avoid negative possibilities, but we also miss the excitement and joy that come from positive outcomes.

That joy was addressed in Gerald Jampolsky's book of personal transformation, *Love Is Letting Go of Fear* (1981), providing a brilliant comparison between the forces of love and fear. Jampolsky, the founder of Attitudinal Healing, wrote:

Fear distorts our perception and confuses what is going on. Love is the total absence of fear. Love asks no questions. Its natural state is one of extension and expansion, not comparison and measurement.

Jampolsky concluded that love is more valuable than fear. Is Jampolsky correct, or is this an unrealistic sonnet ripped from the pages of the book of kumbaya, something that sounds good but falls short? In the previous chapter, *Fearmongering in the here and now*, we determined that fear holds a winning hand and beats love and joy in the real world. Every tyrant, con artist, and spiritual fraudster knows that and uses it to subjugate the masses.

But some stand tall and refuse to be subjugated!

Dorothy Thompson (1893–1961), the "First Lady of American Journalism," looked into the face of fear with the courage and might of the pen. In one of her articles, she eviscerated Adolph Hitler, the world's most feared dictator. Hitler rose to power as Chancellor of Germany in 1933 and later as Der Führer, the "leader" or "guide." Thompson, a correspondent for the American monthly *Cosmopolitan*, was the first American newswoman to interview him in a face-to-face conversation, later recalling her interview:

He is formless, almost faceless, a man whose countenance is a caricature, a man whose framework seems cartilaginous, without bones. He is inconsequent and voluble, ill-poised, insecure. He is the very prototype of the little man. The eyes alone are notable. Dark gray and hyperthyroid—they have the peculiar shine which often distinguishes geniuses, alcoholics, and hysterics.

But after reading her scathing reports of Nazi anti-Semitism, Hitler sent the Gestapo to order Thompson to leave Germany within 24 hours. She was the first American journalist to be expelled from Nazi

Germany and later, enigmatically focused on the essence of fear, as denoted in numerous quotes:

Fear grows in darkness. If you think there's a bogeyman around, turn on the light. The only force that can overcome an idea and a faith is another and better idea and faith, positively and fearlessly upheld.

Perhaps her most profound quote was, "The most destructive element in the human mind is fear." Thompson, like Lovecraft, Jampolsky, and Vallotton, recognized that the primal beast is always lurking. With flared nostrils and hell-spawned eyes, this terrible doppelgänger, while patiently waiting to rip us apart, provides us with ample warning. It always starts with a feeling of unease and a faint chill tingling down our spine, before spilling into our gut as we "know without knowing the how or why."

Dorothy Thompson sat across from Hitler and in her mind saw a faceless, formless little man. She believed that, "The beast is fierce but can be conquered."

"Facing it, always facing it, that's the way to get through. Face it," said Polish-born English novelist Joseph Conrad (1857–1924), author of *Heart of Darkness* (1902), which was later made into Stanley Kubrik's classic, *Apocalypse Now* (1979).

As I write this book, I anticipate being called a fearmonger or worse. In defense, I am merely trying to understand how this most powerful of emotions controls individuals and societies. In my previous book, *Coal Region Hoodoo*, I explored the realm of "Ripperology" and the extremely popular Jack the Ripper cult. How has this fascination over a serial killer from Victorian England held its grip far into the 21st century? And why? It is my belief that Ripperology is another example of Apocalyptic Awe, another way for us to fearlessly look into the eyes of the monster. I will not repeat the information found in *Coal Region Hoodoo*, but, if you are interested in pursuing my exploration into the dark wormhole of fear, then consider *Coal Region Hoodoo* as a good source for that information.

Although fear can push us into past or future gloom, it also provides an opportunity to shift focus to the present and the power of now. We need to ask, what makes one person thrive in the aftermath of adversity, while another suffers? In her article *The Science of Bouncing Back*, *Time's* Mandy Oaklander observed that certain individuals have a unique asset:

> *Resilience is essentially a set of skills—as opposed to a disposition or personality type—that make it possible for people not only to get through hard times but to thrive during and after them. Just as rubber rebounds after being squeezed or squished, so do resilient people.*

Through detailed interviews, research, and MRI scans, neuroscientists found that some individuals handle stress better than others, strengthening connections regulating subcortical fear circuits. In basic terms, the prefrontal cortex (the part of the brain responsible for cognition and planning) communicates to the amygdala (part of the limbic system that responds to perceived threats) that there is no danger and that it needs to settle down. Actively confronting the things that scare you helps relax the fear circuitry, making that an excellent first step in building resilience. Other factors like having a tight-knit community, a stable role model, and a strong belief in one's ability to solve problems help bring about more positive outcomes.

Emotional states can imprison us if we do not address them honestly, as suggested by therapists John Bradshaw, Claudia Black, and Brene Brown. Engaging in Apocalyptic Awe, transforming fear into fascination, allows us to render our demons less threatening. Pastor Chris Vallotton, co-founder of the Bethel School of Supernatural Ministry (BSSM) and Moral Revolution (which empowers you to become a walking encounter with God), observed, "You can't conquer what you refuse to confront."

Life is filled with trade-offs. The big one is about fear. Do we allow it to own us, or do we become mighty soldiers who prepare for battle? We can reach a transformative plane, light years beyond survival, but must first unsheathe our father's sword and lop off the head of the primal beast. That is the *only* way to enjoy a life of joy, courage, and example.

24

THE GLIMMER OF PROMISE

The apocalypse—another name for Lovecraft's crawling chaos—never disappears. In the dimmed light of self-fulfilling prophecy, the rotted corpse of the apocalypse curses us into believing in its inevitability. It is always in our heads, the orphaned byproduct of a toxic culture blathering about zombies, mutants, and serial killers waiting to break inside, and, with a blade to our throat, bind us in duct tape before the inexorable, inevitable end.

Fear can drive us mad as we bask in its refracted glow, but it is a response we can switch on and off. It is a ghost ship without physical properties and a demon conjured through skewed perception. It is only an amorphous concept that is as real or unreal as we make it. The apocalyptical connects us to ancient wisdom and possible catastrophes. It may be relevant as an educational tool, but many unnecessarily obsess over the end times. Doomscrolling, or aimlessly browsing the internet for negative news, is rampant in today's era of electronic messaging, talk radio, and conspiracy theorists. Doomscrolling can provide educational benefits when used in moderation. But a casual habit can turn into a problem when it begins to dominate your life and cause concern. As we plunge into the depths, doomscrolling hijacks our brain in a repetition that traps us in a cycle of despair. It rips away our breath and stomps on our spirit with a monster's jackboot. Instead of making positive changes and reframing neurotic thinking, doomscrollers become dependent upon these soundbites of despondency, like an addict's drug of choice.

A recent study reaffirms the driving curiosity we all share. There is a need for us to know what lies in store, to discover the secret and decipher the code. We are human masters of the puzzle. A 2025 report from the Pew Research Center indicated nearly a third of U.S. adults consult astrology, tarot cards, or fortune tellers at least once a year, with the share highest among young women. Like many things, it can be good or not so good, and, in due course, we need to decide if we really need to see the other side of the tarot card.

With that curiosity in mind, it is possible to determine why specific individuals are likely to be exploited by false prophets and internet trolls. Many individuals exist in an empty shell, feeling unfulfilled—not living, not flourishing, but merely surviving. Like ancient mariners, they fear they will plunge into the abyss but pray that a messianic savior will rescue them. That desperation is the beginning of the end. Every pot has a lid, and every master enslaves a person hardwired to slavishly obey and willing to exchange autonomy for submission.

Life is filled with pain and suffering, mundane existence, and self-doubt, stalking us like desert jackals. Most will taste bitter defeat and reap not the reward but the frustrations of their toil. We endlessly embrace failure and walk upon a familiar pathway, dancing on the edges of death. Fear, anger, and disillusionment are the goblins behind our misery, and we have been reminded of our lot for thousands of years, as foretold in Revelation 9:1-21:

> During those days, people will seek death but will not find it: they will long to die, but death will elude them.

On the surface, a lot of this simply doesn't make sense. Why did the Millerites follow William Miller and continue to embrace the anticipated pain and suffering of the apocalypse? Although the Millerite vision ended in deception, William Miller's influence continued as the Seventh-day Adventists grew out of his philosophies with an emphasis on the promise of the end times and the pain of knowing. These congregants long for the endless nights where they will witness the fire of God that will cleanse the Earth and consume Satan and his angels. Following a strict adherence to the Bible, they observe Saturday as their sabbath and abstain from alcohol, tobacco, and drugs. In 2023, a world membership of 23 million Adventists was reported.

Fear of the apocalypse conjures feelings of hopelessness and despair, with the stare of a dying animal in our eyes. Astrophysicist Carl Sagan predicted that fear would poison the minds of an uneducated populace in the future. His *The Demon-Haunted World: Science as a Candle in the Dark* (1995) encouraged individuals to practice critical and skeptical thinking and differentiate between science and pseudoscience. Sagan used the acronym FEAR (False Evidence Appearing Real), referring to misconceptions or irrational fears based on misleading information, such as mysterious lights or objects we think we see in the sky or the belief that the end times are here. The fear of the unknown, of being unable to find answers and fill in the blanks, leaves us in a state of apprehension, fearing what lies ahead. Because the psyche does not allow for emptiness, the void must be filled with something—confabulation, hallucination, pareidolia, angels, or devils.

Something. Anything.

And that is precisely when irrational thought shifts towards pseudoscience. It doesn't have to. Sagan encourages us to question, seek evidence, and engage in rational discourse. Human problem-solving capabilities and critical thinking can steer us away from scenarios of fear as we seek our center and demand the truth. One finds counsel and therapy in intellectual detachment and analytical thinking. Understanding the parameters of the apocalypse helps us make sense of a rapidly changing technological, multi-cultural world. This disorganized system breathes contradictions of hope and cynicism, heaven and hell.

Life is a constant flux of changes and individual choices. We have the cognition and free will to make our own decisions and survey both sides of the divide. On that score, psychotherapist Nancy Colier, author of *Inviting a Monkey to Tea* (2014), believes that fear can offer both rationality and usefulness:

> *The mind tries to protect us from the fear of what could happen by creating a certainty of what will happen, which paradoxically can feel less frightening.*

At times, it is advisable to see through another perspective, as beauty lies in the eyes of the beholder. Award-winning author and social justice activist L.R. Knost provided a crash course in understanding the bittersweet cynicism:

> *Life is amazing. And then it's awful. And then it's amazing again. And in between the amazing and awful it's ordinary and mundane and routine. Breathe in the amazing, hold on through the awful, and relax and exhale during the ordinary. That's just living heart-breaking, soul-healing, amazing, awful, ordinary life. And it's breathtakingly beautiful.*

We can embrace that beauty but must first confront the source of our pain. Pain is an excellent, yet harsh, teacher, and although humans struggle against the odds, hope springs eternal for those who persevere. In his epic *Desiderata* (1927), American poet Max Ehrmann (1872–1945) offered a list of suggestions for living a satisfying life, leaving his best advice for last:

Therefore, be at peace with God, whatever you conceive Him to be, and whatever your labors and aspirations, in the noisy confusion of life keep peace with your soul. With all its sham, drudgery, and broken dreams, it is still a beautiful world.

Success is about acknowledging failure as a victory, falling forward, and rewarding ourselves with wisdom and insight. The apocalypse represents not only a challenge but also an opportunity for growth, which is what mythologist Joseph Campbell called a "privilege.":

Any disaster you can survive is an improvement in your character, your stature, and your life. What a privilege! Then, when looking back at your life, you will see that the moments which seemed to be great failures followed by wreckage were the incidents that shaped the life you have now. The crisis throws you back, and when you are required to exhibit strength, it comes.

Some argue that fear of the apocalypse is an outdated concept that does not reflect modern times but only distracts us from reality, shifting focus onto dreadful possibilities. That may be true, but for specific individuals and religious groups, the fear is persistent, festering in the slime as a living organism that has to be dealt with in one way or another.

If anything frightens us, it is always based on the fear of the unknown, as articulated by horror master H.P. Lovecraft. This idea has been repeated countless times and represents a central theme of this book. Perhaps the most incomprehensible horror is the thought of looking down into the casket, seeing our pale corpse, and feeling the sadness, detachment, and finality of it all. We hear the voices of the dead, the people we have loved and hated, have helped and harmed, as we are covered in a cascade of guilt and loss. And then the unending darkness.

Ultimately, the apocalypse may represent a therapeutic balm that can heal our fear. The key is to externalize our fears and lock them away. It is easier to watch others die during a catastrophic event, safely from the comfort of our cozy living rooms, than it is to confront our mortality. Observing war, global destruction, and pandemics feels more manageable than facing our death. These events are less personal and do not carry the same intensity that lies at our core.

The end times represent a cluster of toxic ideas that have either invited themselves into our head or accepted our invitation. They are empty of promise and hollow of mood, promoted through unending religious and secular messages, and especially through the excesses of Apocalyptic Awe. To that point, it doesn't matter if these thoughts are imagined or have been learned. What is essential is that they are in our heads, as observed by self-styled "philosophical entertainer" Alan Watts:

> We seldom realize, for example, that our most private thoughts and emotions are not actually our own. For we think in terms of languages and images that we did not invent but which were given to us by our society.

Watts, author of the iconoclastic Beat Zen, Square Zen and Zen (1958), was correct. We are the composite of all the clutter, noise, and swinging monkeys that rumble inside our brains. Originality is a nebulous and elusive concept. We mirror, imitate, and internalize ideas experienced in the world. They may be good or bad, healthy or fractured, or a little of both. Our parents, siblings, and classmates teach us. And like a moth to a flame, we are also taught by the Apocalyptic Awe. Filled with both dread and anticipation, and sometimes mixed with fear and surprise, we are drawn to its essence. Apocalyptic Awe masquerades as entertainment as cultural icons shape our ideas of the world and how we fit in. We try these ideas as a means of being accepted. If a popular heavy metal star sports tattoos on their neck and wears skin-tight leather outfits and chains, that persona may be our key to being accepted.

However, to rise above the fray and be an independent thinker, perhaps in the pathways of Henry David Thoreau, Ralph Waldo Emerson, John Muir, and Walt Whitman, takes a confident and independent-minded individual. Those with a poor sense of self will accept the pseudoscience embedded in conspiracy theories promoting dystopian fear.

Pseudoscience proclamations are as deceptive as the day is long. Examples are too numerous to be listed appropriately but include Hillary Clinton's "Pizzagate," sightings of Elvis, the Roswell and Kecksburg UFO crashes, the resurrections of President John F. Kennedy and John Kennedy Jr., and other gibberish spewed from the slime-encrusted mouth of the apocalypse. Examples of this junk science mumbo jumbo are equivalent to chimpanzees throwing feces against a blank canvas. But, incongruously, all of these fecal masterpieces rent space in the minds of the beholders. No matter what the conspiracy, someone will step forward, raise their hand, and proclaim, "Yes. This is true. I know it's true because the Deep State and the government are lying to us. They are hiding something from us."

Consider that a little bit of truth can be dangerous, because a kernel of truth is always hidden within the conspiracy, lending a sliver of credibility to the search for meaning. Equally dangerous is when we betray ourselves and, looking into the mirror, see Judas Iscariot staring back. Rather than using critical, evidence-based thinking, we allow others to choose the topics and dialogue. We are passive and not active participants. Steven Covey would be so proud of us, as we are among the world's greatest listeners.

Is the apocalypse inevitable, or only a bedtime story taught since infancy? In any case, what is the counterpoint to all this horror? There are other questions equally important. We are human. We live, create, find joy, and then we die. But if this is our final act, shouldn't it be one of adventure and courage, like Erik Erikson's wide-eyed child exploring the universe for the first time. Will death grant us a glimmer of promise and allow a smile on our face, and, in addition, if there is justice in the world, will that be our ultimate reward? Are we doomed to suffer the fever of the damned, or is there something more magnificent in store for us?

In our youthful dreams we sought to climb mountains and build lofty mansions that touched the edge of heaven—before learning the lessons of illusion and reality. Only a few will grasp the golden ring and taste success. Others will be seduced into a belief that somehow things will magically and effortlessly get better. The reality is that life rarely unfolds as we expect. What most savor and cradle to their breasts are hallucinatory dreams promising greener grasses and castles in the sky, but lacking hard work. Success can only be attained by those who want it, stay the course, and are guided by destiny's hand. Hard work and perseverance are essential for success. You control your fate.

Every day, I meditate, exercise, read, write, research, and attend to the things that bring joy and fulfillment. It's all about doing the work again and again. The formula is to be a juggler: keep spinning balls in the air, waiting for that point of synchronicity where destiny embraces our energies and acknowledges our accomplishments.

No matter how heavy the days, don't lose faith, because brighter, gentler days *are* coming. Keep your eyes on the prize. Don't stop, and know that your power rests in the present moment and not in the future. Choose "the power of now," as spiritual teacher Eckhart Tolle instructed, and remember that because the pathway is the same for all of us, we need to support and inspire each other.

Thank you for reading this book. Long months were spent researching and writing in hopes that it would be a positive experience for you, the reader. Authors exist in a twilight zone where silence and a lack of feedback seem to be the norm. If you have thoughts about this book, please consider posting a review on Amazon or Goodreads, the authors' lifeline.

In closing, may joy find you in the most unexpected ways and hope light your path. May your shadow never diminish as you escape the clutches of the devil and the apocalypse's wrath.

Until we meet on the pathway.
Maxim W. Furek, 2025

ACKNOWLEDGMENTS

Thanks to the Citrus Writers of Florida's Paula Braley and Donna Consiglio and for their support and proofreading skills. Thanks to minimalist poet John Yamrus for his amazingly keen eye and faster-than-the-speed-of-light feedback.

REFERENCES

2: Exordium & Terminus

A 2025 report from the Pew Research Center indicates nearly a third of U.S. adults consult astrology, tarot cards or fortune tellers at least. Pew Research May 21, 2025. https://www.pewresearch.org/religion/2025/05/21/3-in-10-americans-consult-astrology-tarot-cards-or-fortune-tellers/

Abbott, Brianna. The Chilling Song That Dominated the Charts During the Moon Landing. Wall Street Journal. July 14, 2019. https://www.wsj.com/articles/the-chilling-song-that-dominated-the-charts-during-the-moon-landing-11563152401

Armstrong, Sam. Lady Gaga and Bruno Mars Crack Billion YouTube Views For 'Die With a Smile'. U. Discover Music. May 6, 2025. https://www.udiscovermusic.com/news/lady-gaga-bruno-mars-die-with-a-smile-billion-youtube/

Beviglia, Jim. The Story and Meaning Behind "The End of the World," an All-Time Weeper from Country Legend Skeeter Davis. American Songwriter. September 16, 2024. https://americansongwriter.com/the-story-and-meaning-behind-the-end-of-the-world-an-all-time-weeper-from-country-legend-skeeter-davis/

Farrant, Dan. 22 of The Best Songs About the End of the World. Hello Music Theory. October 10, 2023. https://hellomusictheory.com/learn/songs-about-the-end-of-the-world/

Meyer, Isabella. Four Horsemen of the Apocalypse Dürer – An Analysis. Art in Context. August 1, 2023. https://artincontext.org/four-horsemen-of-the-apocalypse-durer/

Nassim, Mayer. 'In The Year 2525' by Zager and Evans: The making of the chart-topping sci-fi masterpiece. Gold Radio. July 3, 2023. https://www.goldradio.com/features/song-facts/in-the-year-2525-zager-evans-lyrics-meaning/

Neary, Lynn. 'Grapes Of Wrath' And the Politics of Book Burning. NPR. September 30, 2008. https://www.npr.org/2008/09/30/95190615/grapes-of-wrath-and-the-politics-of-book-burning

Reynolds, Tom. I Hate Myself and Want to Die: The 52 Most Depressing Songs You've Ever Heard. Milsons Point, N.S.W.: Random House. 2005.

Steinbeck, John. The Grapes of Wrath. New York: The Viking Press. 1939.

Strauss, Neil. After the Horror, Radio Stations Pull Some Songs. The New York Times. September 19, 2001.

The Four Horsemen, from "The Apocalypse." Albrecht Dürer, German. The Met. May 29, 2025. https://www.metmuseum.org/art/collection/search/336215

The Story behind the Song "In the Year 2525." (Exordium & Terminus). By Zager and Evans. Philistine. August 23, 2023. https://www.philistineband.com/post/the-story-behind-the-song

References

The Art and Symbolism of Revelation Through the Ages. AB Renens.May 29, 2025. https://ab-renens.ch/the-art-and-symbolism-of-revelation-through-the-ages/

Wilton, Emma. Books Like 1984: Must-Read Dystopian Novels. Epic Books. December 10, 2024. https://epicbooks.app/blog/books-like-1984

3: HP Lovecraft

Bauer, Patricia. Cthulhu. *Britannica*. October 22, 2023. https://www.britannica.com/topic/Cthulhu

Cain, Sian. Ten Things You Should Know about HP Lovecraft. *The Guardian*. August 20, 2014. https://www.theguardian.com/books/2014/aug/20/ten-things-you-should-know-about-hp-lovecraft

DeLaughter, John. Lovecraft's Cthulhu and the Great Old Ones: Fact, Fiction or Foretold in the Necronomicon? The Lovecraft eZine. August 22, 2016. https://lovecraftzine.com/2016/07/21/lovecrafts-cthulhu-and-the-great-old-ones-fact-fiction-or-foretold-in-the-necronomicon/

Fox, Alex. Nearly 2,000 Black Americans Were Lynched During Reconstruction. A new report brings the number of victims of racial terror killings between 1865 and 1950 to almost 6,500. Smithsonian. June 18, 2020. https://www.smithsonianmag.com/smart-news/nearly-2000-black-americans-were-lynched-during-reconstruction-180975120/

Furek, Maxim W. Howard Phillips Lovecraft: The Haunter in the Dark. *Fate*. April 2024. 740, 34-29.

Gurzo, Miranda. When the Stars Will Be Right: HP Lovecraft Between Prophecy and Apocalypse. *Axis Mundi*. June 18, 2020. https://axismundi.blog/en/2020/06/18/when-the-stars-will-be-right-hp-lovecraft-between-prophecy-and-apocalypse/

Joshi, Sunand T. Howard Phillips Lovecraft: The Life of a Gentleman of Providence. *Biograph*. April 29, 2023. https://www.hplovecraft.com/life/biograph.aspx

Oates, Joyce Carol. (Ed.) *Tales of H.P. Lovecraft*. The New York: Ecco Press. 1997.

Root, Damon. The Uncanny Afterlife of H.P. Lovecraft. *Reason*. January 2020. https://reason.com/2019/12/27/the-uncanny-afterlife-of-h-p-lovecraft/

Stefansky, Emma. A monsterous primer on the works of H.P. Lovecraft. August 23, 2018. https://www.polygon.com/2018/8/23/17762378/hp-lovecraft-books-cthulhu-necronomicon-stories

Soloski, Alexis. Gods, Monsters and H.P. Lovecraft's Uncanny Legacy. *New York Times*. August 7, 2020. https://www.nytimes.com/2020/08/07/arts/television/hp-lovecraft.html

Somers, Jeffrey. Biography of H.P. Lovecraft, American Writer, Father of Modern Horror. *Thought.Co*. March 27, 2020. https://www.thoughtco.com/biography-of-h-p-lovecraft-american-writer-4800728

Sprague de Camp, L. Lovecraft: A Biography. Garden City, NY: Doubleday & Company, Inc. 1975.

Tulfo, Erika. Books like 'The Handmaid's Tale' and '1984' are flying off the shelves after

the presidential election. CNN. November 7, 2024. https://www.cnn.com/2024/11/07/
business/1984-handmaids-tale-books-election/index.html

4: The Bridge to the Apocalypse

Browne, Sylvia and Harrison, Lindsay. The End of Days: Predictions and Prophecies
About the End of the World. New York: Berkley. 2009.

Chua, Amy. Political Tribes: Group Instinct and the Fate of Nations. London: Penguin
Press. 2019.

Greer, John Michael. Apocalypse: A History of the End of Time. London: Queros. 2012.

Hamill, Jasper. We're in an age of 'apocalypse anxiety' and will never stop worrying
about doomsday. *Metro*. June 7, 2019. https://metro.co.uk/2019/06/07/age-apoca
lypse-anxiety-will-never-stop-worrying-doomsday-9853553/

Hesse, Hermann. Steppenwolf: A Novel. New York: Picador. 1929.

Revelation 19:11-16. BibleGateWay. December 6, 2024. https://www.biblegateway.com/
passage/?search=Revelation%2019:11-16&version=KJV

Santayana, George (1863-1952). Harvard Square Library. November 6, 2024. https://www.
harvardsquarelibrary.org/cambridge-harvard/george-santayana/

Sapolsky, Robert. The 2% Difference. Now that scientists have decoded the chim-
panzee genome, we know that 98 percent of our DNA is the same. So how can we
be so different? Discover. May 20, 2025. https://www.discovermagazine.com/planet-
earth/the-2-difference

Sarkar, Donna. 20 Brilliant Quotes from Albert Einstein, the Theoretical Physicist Who
Became World Famous. Discovery. March 14, 2013. https://www.discovermagazine.
com/the-sciences/20-brilliant-quotes-from-albert-einstein-the-theoretical-physi
cist-who

Solly, Meilan. The Real History Behind 'The Zone of Interest' and Rudolf Höss.
History. January 4, 2024. https://www.smithsonianmag.com/history/the-real-
history-behind-the-zone-of-interest-and-rudolf-hoss-180983531/

Steinberg, Alan J. Symmetry, Beauty, and Wisdom: Qualities Shaping Our Universe.
Psychology Today. May 27, 2023. https://www.psychologytoday.com/us/blog/the-
meditating-mind/202305/symmetry-beauty-and-wisdom-qualities-shaping-our-
universe

The Fall by Albert Camus. Allegory Explained. June 5, 2025. https://allegoryexplained.
com/the-fall/

The Last Man on Earth.1964. IMDb. December 6, 2024. https://www.imdb.com/title/
tt0058700/

The Last Man on Earth. Public Domain Movies. May 27, 2025. https://publicdomain
movie.net/movie/the-last-man-on-earth

Holland, T. *Apocalypse: A History of the End of Times*.

Wells, H.G. The Island of Dr. Moreau. London: Heinemann. 1896.

5: The Doomsday Clock

Chappell, Bill. What happens now after Russia suspends the last nuclear arms treaty with the U.S.? NPR. February 22, 2023. https://www.npr.org/2023/02/22/1158529106/nuclear-treaty-new-start-putin

Good, Christopher. An economic meltdown is the doomsday Americans fear the most. Here's why. Ipsos.com. April 8, 2024. https://www.ipsos.com/en-us/economic-meltdown-doomsday-americans-fear-most-heres-why

Haynes, Deborah. World entering a new nuclear age, head of armed forces warns. Sky News. December 4, 2024. https://news.sky.com/story/world-entering-a-new-nuclear-age-head-of-armed-forces-warns-13266960?dcmp=snt-sf-twitter

Kelvey, Jon. Does the Doomsday Clock actually mean anything? Experts weigh in. Inverse. January 29, 2003. https://www.inverse.com/science/is-the-doomsday-clock-legit

Kristensen, Hans M. (2023). Status Of World Nuclear Forces. Bulletin of the Atomic Scientists. 79 (1): 28–52.

Maslin, Mark. Nuclear war would be more devastating for Earth's climate than cold war predictions – even with fewer weapons. The Conversation. August 1, 2023. https://theconversation.com/nuclear-war-would-be-more-devastating-for-earths-climate-than-cold-war-predictions-even-with-fewer-weapons-210567

Mecklin, John. It is *still* 90 seconds to midnight. 2024 Doomsday Clock Statement. *Bulletin of the Atomic Scientists.* January 23, 2024. https://thebulletin.org/doomsday-clock/current-time/

Pompliano, Polina. The Profile Dossier: Christopher Nolan, the Visionary Behind Cinema's Best Psychological Thrillers. The Profile. April 21, 2021. https://www.readtheprofile.com/p/christopher-nolan

Richardson, Hannah, "The End of the World: Fear of the Apocalypse" (2019). *Student Scholar Symposium Abstracts and Posters.* 345. https://digitalcommons.chapman.edu/cusrd_abstracts/345

Robinson, Kali. What is the Iran Nuclear Deal? Council on Foreign Relations. October 27, 2023. https://www.cfr.org/backgrounder/what-iran-nuclear-deal

7: Apocalyptic Awe

Ballard, J.G. The Drowned World. New York: Liveright Publishing Corporation. 1962.

Bauer, Pat., and Cregan-Reid, Vybarr. Gulliver's Travels novel by Swift. Encyclopaedia Britannica. April 21, 2025. https://www.britannica.com/topic/Gullivers-Travels

Bell, Art, and Strieber, Whitley. The Coming Global Superstorm. New York: Pocket Books. 1999.

Burgess, Anthony. A Clockwork Orange. London: William Heinemann. 1962.

Chin, Daniel. What You Need to Know Before Watching '28 Years Later'
The Ringer. June 18, 2025. https://www.theringer.com/2025/06/18/movies/28-years-later-primer-28-days-later-danny-boyle-alex-garland

Dolan, Leah. This is all pink and attractive, but we are going to die': Anastasia Samoylova on photographing Florida's climate anxiety. CNN. December 9, 2024. https://www.yahoo.com/news/pink-attractive-going-die-anastasia-110106552.html

Jonathan Swift and the moons of Mars. David Darling. June 5, 2025. https://www.david darling.info/encyclopedia/S/Swift.html

Kidd C, Hayden BY. The Psychology and Neuroscience of Curiosity. Neuron. 2015 Nov 4;88(3):449-6c. doi: 10.1016/j.neuron.2015.09.010. PMID: 26539887; PMCID: PMC4635443.

McCloud, Cheryl. Florida just ties record with 3 hurricanes making landfall in single year. Hurricane Milton become the third hurricane to make landfall in Florida in 2024. USA Today. October 21, 2024. https://www.jacksonville.com/story/weather/hurricane/2024/10/18/florida-hurricanes-debby-helene-milton-tie-record-landfalls/75718304007/

Neikirk, Todd. Kurt Vonnegut's Time as a Soldier During WWII Inspired His Popular Anti-War Novel, 'Slaughterhouse-Five.' War History Online. March 24, 2022. https://www.warhistoryonline.com/category/war-articles

Nuclear Tourism: When atomic tests were a tourist attraction in Las Vegas, 1950s. Rare Historic Photos. June 14, 2025. https://rarehistoricalphotos.com/atomic-tourism-las-vegas/

The Forgotten Author Who Predicted the Sinking of the Titanic. Interesting Literature. June 6, 2025. https://interestingliterature.com/2020/11/titanic-sinking-novel-predicted-robertson/

Titanic. History.com. May 28, 2025. https://www.history.com/articles/titanic

Vonnegut Jr., Kurt. Slaughterhouse-Five, or, The Children's Crusade: A Duty-Dance with Death. New York: Delacorte: 1969.

Wilson, Teresa. This Month in Astronomical History: The Moons of Mars. US Naval Obsevertory, Historical Astronomy Division. August 2016. https://aas.org/posts/story/2016/07/month-astronomical-history-moons-mars

8 & 9: The Masque of the Red Death

1968 flu pandemic. Encyclopedia Britannica, November 18, 2024. https://www.britannica.com/facts/1968-flu-pandemic.

Africa: Conflicts, Violence Threaten Rights. Improve Civilian Protection, Accountability for Abuses. *Human Rights Watch*. January 12, 2023. https://www.hrw.org/news/2023/01/12/africa-conflicts-violence-threaten-rights

Akpan, Nsikan. America's HIV outbreak started in this city, 10 years before anyone noticed. PBS Science. October 26, 2016. https://www.pbs.org/newshour/science/america-hiv-outbreak-origins-nyc-gaetan-dugas

Aleccia, J. CDC calls for expanded testing for bird flu after blood tests reveal more farmworker infections. *PBS News*. (November 7, 2024). https://www.pbs.org/newshour/health/cdc-calls-for-expanded-testing-for-bird-flu-after-blood-tests-reveal-more-farmworker-infections

Aryal, Sagar. Biosafety Levels (BSL-1, BSL-2, BSL-3 and BSL-4). Microbe Notes. June 16, 2022. https://microbenotes.com/biosafety-levels/

Avian Influenza (Bird Flu.) CDC. June 1, 2024. ht

Barber, Carolyn. Yahoo.com. February 8, 2025. New bird flu variant found in Nevada dairy cows has experts sounding alarms: 'We have never been closer to a pandemic from this virus'. https://www.yahoo.com/news/bird-flu-variant-found-nevada-034706069.html

Black Death. *History.* March 28, 2023. https://www.history.com/topics/middle-ages/black-death

CDC A(H5N1) Bird Flu Response Update. November 4, 2024. *CDC.* https://www.cdc.gov/bird-flu/spotlights/h5n1-response-11012024.html.

Cervantes Jr., Fernando. Where has the bird flu spread across the US? USA Today. February 7, 2025. https://www.yahoo.com/news/where-bird-flu-spread-across-205703595.html

Diphtheria. World Health Organization. July 12, 2024. https://www.who.int/news-room/fact-sheets/detail/diphtheria

Doucleff, M. So, you think you know all about the plague? *NPR News.* February 14, 2024. https://www.npr.org/sections/goatsandsoda/2024/02/14/1231215446/so-you-think-you-know-all-about-the-plague

Horgan, John. World History Encyclopedia. December 26, 2014. https://www.worldhistory.org/article/782/justinians-plague-541-542-ce/

Justinian's Plague: History and Major Facts. World History EDU. December 8, 2024. https://worldhistoryedu.com/justinians-plague/

Kee, Caroline. Why is this year's flu season so bad? Doctors weigh in on symptoms and prevention. Yahoo.com. February 12, 2025. https://www.yahoo.com/news/why-flu-season-bad-doctors-093428478.html

Kolata, Gina. Flu: The Story of The Great Influenza Pandemic of 1918 and the Search for the Virus that Caused It. New York: Atria. 1999.

LDH reports first U.S. H5N1-related human death. Louisiana Department of Health. January 6, 2025. https://ldh.la.gov/news/H5N1-death?utm_source=join1440&utm_medium=email&utm_placement=newsletter

Martichoux, Alix. Fungus labeled 'urgent threat' by CDC is spreading rapidly, hospital study finds. The Hill. March 22, 2025 https://www.yahoo.com/news/fungus-labeled-urgent-threat-cdc-130000001.html

Matsumoto, G. *Vaccine A.* New York: Basic Books. 2004.

Mpox. *World Health Organization.* August 26, 202). https://www.who.int/news-room/fact-sheets/detail/mpox

Nix, Jessica and Smith, Gerry. US Investigates Worrying Bird Flu Strain on Duck Farm in California. Yahoo.com. January 27, 2025. https://www.yahoo.com/finance/news/us-investigates-worrying-bird-flu-204520047.html

Oishimaya, Sen Nag. Infectious Diseases That Have Been Globally Eradicated. World Atlas. June 27, 2018. https://www.worldatlas.com/articles/infectious-diseases-that-have-been-globally-eradicated.html

Ornell F, Schuch JB, Sordi AO, Kessler FHP. "Pandemic fear" and COVID-19: mental health burden and strategies. Braz J Psychiatry. 2020;00:000-000. http://dx.doi.org/ 10.1590/1516-4446-2020-0008

Poe's Stories: *The Masque of the Red Death*. LitCharts. November 9, 2024. https://www. litcharts.com/lit/poe-s-stories/the-masque-of-the-red-death

Pope, Carmen. 7 Deadliest Diseases in History: Where are they now? Drugs.com. May 14, 2023. https://www.drugs.com/medical-answers/7-deadliest-diseases-history-3573756/

Pryor, E.R. "The Great Plague of Hong Kong," Journal of the Royal Asiatic Society Hong Kong, 63, 15. © History Society A.A.H.K.U. Publications and its authors

Rogers, K. "Influenza pandemic (H1N1) of 2009." *Encyclopedia Britannica*. April 15, 2024. m https://www.britannica.com/event/influenza-pandemic-H1N1-of-2009.

Shastri, Devi. The tuberculosis outbreak in Kansas is alarming. It's not the biggest in US history though, CDC says. Washington Post. January 28, 2025. https://www.wash ingtonpost.com/health/2025/01/28/tuberculosis-tb-outbreak-kansas-largest/ 0f7ee360-ddc8-11ef-8889-d5c3924edafd_story.html

Stobbe, M. STD epidemic slows as new syphilis, gonorrhea cases fall in U.S. *Associated Press*. November 13, 2024.

The History of AIDS in Africa. Black History Month. August 25, 2015. https://www. blackhistorymonth.org.uk/article/section/real-stories/the-history-of-aids-in-africa/

The Masque of the Red Death. *Poe Stories*. November 10, 2024. https://poestories.com/ read/masque

Ungar, Laura. CDC: Bird flu virus likely mutated in LA. Associated Press. December 28, 2024.

10 & 11: The Doomsday Fish

1972- Hurricane Agnes. National Weather service. January 7, 2025. https://www.weather. gov/bgm/pastFloodJune1972

Allen, William Rodney. A Brief Biography of Kurk Vonnegut. Vonnegut Library. January 12, 2025. https://www.vonnegutlibrary.org/biography/

Bailey, Regina. Life in the Mesopelagic Zone of the Ocean: The Ocean's Twilight Zone. ThoughtCo. July 3, 2019. https://www.thoughtco.com/mesopelagic-zone-4685646

Bell, Art and Strieber, Whitley. The Coming Global Superstorm. New York City: Atria Books. 1999.

Borenstein, Seth. World is pumping out 57 million tons of plastic pollution a year. PhysOrg. September 8, 2024. https://phys.org/news/2024-09-world-million-tons-plastic- pollution.html

Borenstein, Seth, and Arusu, Sibi. A US state is sixth in the world for pollution, according to climate scientists. Nation World. November 15, 2024. https://www.wtol. com/article/news/nation-world/most-polluting-cities/507-f3590c42-0db9-4f50-9219-896436cefcof

Bryant, Chloe. Scientist makes startling discovery at Earth's deepest point: 'What a disgusting and embarrassing display.' Yahoo!life. January 9, 2025. https://www.

yahoo.com/lifestyle/scientist-makes-startling-discovery-earths-103017789.html?.
tsrc=fp_deeplink

Donaldson James, Susan. Apocalypse Now: Floods, Tornadoes, Locusts: Is violent weather around the globe a sign of a coming Apocalypse?" ABC News. June 13, 2008. https://abcnews.go.com/US/Weather/story?id=5062583&page=1

Dunn, Betty. What Do Locusts Represent in the Bible and in the End Times? Cross-Walk. March 2, 2021. https://www.crosswalk.com/faith/bible-study/what-do-locusts-represent-in-the-bible-and-in-the-end-times.html

Dust Bowl. Britannica. March 27, 2025. https://www.britannica.com/place/Dust-Bowl

"Dusty Old Dust," (So Long, It's Been Good to Know Yuh). Written by Woody Guthrie." Copywrite 1940 (renewed),1951 (renewed) by Woody Guthrie Publications. Inc. & TRO-Ludlow Music, Inc. (BMI).

Dyck, Bruce. Dirty Thirties: fact and myth. The Western Producer. July 28,2005. https://www.producer.com/news/dirty-thirties-fact-and-myth/

George, Stephen C. Meet the Doomsday Fish that Strikes Fear in the Hearts of Sailors. Discovery. June 18, 2024. https://www.discovermagazine.com/planet-earth/meet-the-doomsday-fish-that-strikes-fear-in-the-hearts-of-sailors

Ghose, Tia. The 12 biggest volcanic eruptions in recorded history. LiveScience. June 10, 2013. https://www.livescience.com/planet-earth/volcanos/the-12-biggest-volcanic-eruptions-in-recorded-history

Harvey, Lex. 'It's as if an atomic bomb fell on Mayotte': Widespread destruction after 100-year cyclone pummels French territory. CNN. December 16, 2024. https://www.yahoo.com/news/atomic-bomb-fell-mayotte-widespread-052349947.html

Heuvelmans, Bernard. The Kraken and the Colossal Octopus. Abingdon: Kegan Paul Limited. 2006.

Jacobo, Julia. Why was the flooding in Ashville, North Carolina, so extreme? Meteorologists explain. ABC News. October 3, 2024. https://abcnews.go.com/US/flooding-asheville-north-carolina-extreme-meteorologists-explain/story?id=114461744

Joshin, RI. Dust Bowl Preachers. November 2024. https://community.logos.com/discussion/131725/dust-bowl-preachers

Larson, Christina. New research shows a quarter of freshwater animals are threatened with extinction. ABC News. January 8, 2025. https://abcnews.go.com/Technology/wireStory/new-research-shows-quarter-freshwater-animals-threatened-extinction-117463763

Lookingbill, Brad. A Gof-Forsaken Place: Folk Eschatology and the Dust Bowl. Great Plains Quarterly. Paper 801.1994. http://digitalcommons.unl.edu/greatplainsquarterly/801

Lomborg, Bjorn. There's a cheaper way to tackle climate change. InsideSources.com. December 13, 2024.

Lott, Maxim. 10 times 'experts' predicted the world would end by now. Fox News. March 9, 2019. https://www.foxnews.com/science/10-times-experts-predicted-the-world-would-end-by-now

M., Anastacia. 10 Deadliest Weather Disasters in History. Rain Viewer. May 9, 2023.

https://www.rainviewer.com/blog/top-10-deadliest-weather-disasters-in-histo
ry.html

MessyNessy. The Ten Year Apocalypse that Nearly Destroyed Midwestern America.
October 8, 2015. https://www.messynessychic.com/2015/04/03/the-ten-year-apoca
lypse-that-inspired-interstellar-and-nearly-destroyed-midwester-america/

Poynting, Mark, Rivault, Erwan, and Dale, Becky. 2024 first year to pass 1.5C global
warming limit. BBC. January 10, 2025. https://www.bbc.com/news/articles/
cd7575x8yq50

Rycroft, Rick. What is a 1 in 100 year weather event? And why do they keep happening
so often? The Conversation. March 22, 2021. https://theconversation.com/what-is-a-
1-in-100-year-weather-event-and-why-do-they-keep-happening-so-often-157589

Sawyer, Dawn. 'Doomsday fish' returns to Southern California shores for the third
time this year. CNN. November 18, 2024. https://www.yahoo.com/news/doomsday-
fish-returns-southern-california-011418621.html

St. John, Alexa. Climate change added 41 days of dangerous heat around world in 2024.
The Detroit News. December 27, 2024. https://www.detroitnews.com/story/news/
world/2024/12/27/climate-change-added-41-days-dangerous-heat-around-world-
2024/77256919007/

The Black Sunday Dust Storm of April 14, 1935. National Weather Service. April 12,
2025. https://www.weather.gov/oun/events-19350414

The Dust Bowl Years. Adams County Nebraska Historical Society. April 15, 2025.
https://www.adamshistory.org/index.php?option=com_content&view=article&id=
18&catid=2

The Grapes of Wrath. Stanford: The Steinbeck Institute. April 14, 2025. https://stein
beck.stanford.edu/grapeshistorical

12 & 13: The Mothman Prophecy

10 Fatal Building Collapses That Have Remained in the Public's Mind for Years. Arch.
February 20, 2025. https://www.arch20.com/10-worst-building-collapses-in-the-
world/

Barker, Gray. The Silver Bridge: The Classic Mothman Tale. Clarksburg, WV:
Saucerian Books. 1970.

Futterman, Allison. 5 Examples of the Worst Human-Made Disasters in History.
Discover. August 5, 2023. https://www.discovermagazine.com/the-sciences/5-exam
ples-of-the-worst-human-made-disasters-in-history

Grabowski, William. The Mothman Fallacies. The Night Run. February 23, 2014.
https://thenightrun.wordpress.com/2014/02/23/the-mothman-fallacies/

Hutchison, Harold. "UFO Mystery Solved: "Mothmen" Were Actually Green Berets."
Soldier of Fortune. 2014.

Jennings, Mike. 10 of the world's biggest man-made disasters. LiveScience. January 18,
2022. https://www.livescience.com/worlds-biggest-man-made-disasters

Jordon. Top 30 Most Astonishing Mining Disasters in History. FTM. February 15, 2023.

https://www.ftmmachinery.com/blog/top-30-most-astonishing-mining-disasters-in-history.html

Kahler, Abbott. What (or Who) Caused the Great Chicago Fire? The true story behind the myth of Mrs. O'Leary and her cow. Smithsonian. October 4, 2012. https://www.smithsonianmag.com/history/what-or-who-caused-the-great-chicago-fire-61481977/

Keel, John. The Mothman Prophesies. New York: Saturday Review Press. 1975.

McNamera, Robert. Did Mrs. O'Leary's Cow Start the Great Chicago Fire? The Facts Behind the Incendiary Legend. ThoughtCo. March 21, 2021. https://www.thoughtco.com/mrs-olearys-cow-great-chicago-fire-1774059

Makoii, Akhtar. Watch: Russian drone blows hole in Chernobyl's protective shell. The Telegraph. February 14, 2025. https://www.yahoo.com/news/watch-russian-drone-blows-hole-110107298.html

Margaritoff, Marco. What Really Happened The Evening The Silver Bridge Collapsed In 1967? AllThatsInteresting.com, August 10, 2024, https://allthatsinteresting.com/silver-bridge-collapse.

Pickering, G.D. *Mysterious Creatures: The Mothman of Point Pleasant: One of America's most famous cryptids alongside Bigfoot & The Michigan Dogman.* 2023.

Smale, Katherine. Insight: The Ronan Point legacy 50 years on. New Civil Engineer. May 16, 2018. https://www.newcivilengineer.com/latest/insight-the-ronan-point-legacy-50-years-on-16-05-2018/

The Silver Bridge Collapses Killing 46. West Virginia Public Broadcasting. December 15, 1967. https://wvpublic.org/the-silver-bridge-collapses-killing-46-december-15-1967/

Whelton, Andrew J. Ohio Train Derailment's Toxic Fallout Lingered in The Worst Possible Places. Science Alert. October 1, 2024. https://www.sciencealert.com/ohio-train-derailments-toxic-fallout-lingered-in-the-worst-possible-places

Wizevich, Eli. A 1903 Fire at a Chicago Theater Killed 602 People, Prompting Enduring Safety Reforms. Smithsonian. December 30, 2024. https://www.smithsonianmag.com/smart-news/a-1903-fire-at-a-chicago-theater-killed-602-people-prompting-enduring-safety-reforms-180985661/

14: The Four Horsemen References

Bolinger, Hope. Who Are the Four Horsemen of the Apocalypse? Christianity. June 21, 2024. https://www.christianity.com/wiki/end-times/who-are-the-four-horsemen-in-revelation-their-meaning-and-significance.html

Fairchild, Mary. What Are the Four Horsemen of the Apocalypse? Learn Religions. October 5, 2024. https://www.learnreligions.com/four-horsemen-of-the-apocalypse-4843887

Grondin, Charles. Who wrote the book of Revelation? Catholic Answers. January 25, 2025. https://www.catholic.com/qa/who-wrote-the-book-of-revelation

Hickson, Sally. Albrecht Dürer, The Four Horsemen of the Apocalypse. Khan Academy. January 24, 2025. https://www.khanacademy.org/humanities/renaissance-reformation/northern/durer/a/drer-the-four-horsemen-of-the-apocalypse

Martin, Roland. Seven Seals. Encyclopaedia Britannica. October 16, 2023. https://www.britannica.comhttps://www.britannica.com/topic/seven-seals

Meyer, Isabella. Four Horsemen of the Apocalypse Dürer – An Analysis. Art in Context. August 1, 2023. https://artincontext.org/four-horsemen-of-the-apocalypse-durer/

Mills, Kenyette. The Great Tribulation: The Four Horsemen of The Apocalypse & The Seven Seals. The God Blog. May 13, 2020. https://thegodblog.org/2020/05/13/the-great-tribulation-the-four-horsemen-of-the-apocalypse-the-seven-seals/

Seven Seals. Bible Hub. June 14, 2025. https://biblehub.com/topical/s/seven_seals.htm

15: Weaponized Religion

Al-Qa' ida. Terrorist Groups. National Counterterrorism Center. April 12, 2025. https://www.dni.gov/nctc/terrorist_groups/al_qaida.html

Aum Shinrikyo: The Japanese cult behind the Tokyo Sarin attack. BBC News. July 6, 2018. https://www.bbc.com/news/world-asia-35975069

Brownfeld, A. C. KOERNER, "HOFFER'S AMERICA," AND HOFFER, "THE TRUE BELIEVER" & "THE TEMPER OF OUR TIME." *Libertarianism.* December 1, 1974. https://www.libertarianism.org/publications/essays/koerner-hoffers-america-hoffer-true-believer-temper-our-time

David Koresh. Biography. March 27, 2023. https://www.biography.com/crime/david-koresh

Fear. Nanda Nursing Diagnosis List. March 29, 2025. http://nandanursingdiagnosislist.org/#google_vignette

Dubrow-Marshall, Linda and Dubrow-Marshall, Rod. How cult leader Charles Manson was able to manipulate his 'family' to commit murder. The Conversation. November 20, 2017. https://theconversation.com/how-cult-leader-charles-manson-was-able-to-manipulate-his-family-to-commit-murder-70961

Furek, Maxim W. Looking into the Face of Fear. *The Sober World*, 5, (12), 14. December 2016.

Italie, Hillel. Salman Rushdie's first book of fiction since his stabbing will be published in November. Associated Press. March 28, 2025.

Hoffer, Eric. The True Believer. New York: Harper & Row, Publishers. 1951.

Huxley, Aldous *The Olive Tree: and other essays*. London: Chatto & Windus. 1947.

Kennedy, William. What Life Inside Prison Is Really Like For Warren Jeffs From Peacock's Preaching Evil. Grunge. June 17, 2022. https://www.grunge.com/840419/what-life-inside-prison-is-really-like-for-warren-jeffs-from-peacocks-preaching-evil/

Miller, E. C. Trump fits 'demagogue' definition. *Press Enterprise*. November 2, 2024. Vol 123, No. 247, 19.

Morrison, E. Why Do Some of Us Look Forward to the End of the World? A Personal Perspective: The dangers of the Apocalypse mindset. Psychology Today. October 21, 2022. https://www.psychologytoday.com/us/blog/word-less/202210/why-do-some-of-us-look-forward-to-the-end-of-the-world

National Scientific Council on the Developing Child 2010. *Persistent Fear and Anxiety Can Affect Young Children's Learning and Development: Working Paper No. 9.* www.developingchild.harvard.edu.

Popper, Karl. The Open Society and Its Enemies. London: Routledge. 1945.

Preparing for the Psychological Consequences of Terrorism: A Public Health Strategy. National Library of Medicine. 2003. https://www.ncbi.nlm.nih.gov/books/NBK221638/

Preparing for the Psychological Consequences of Terrorism: A Public Health Strategy. National Library of Medicine. 2003. https://www.ncbi.nlm.nih.gov/books/NBK221638/

Rose, Sophia. The Spiritual Meaning of Apocalypse: A Journey Beyond Fear. Wisdom of the Spirit. March 29, 2025. https://wisdomofthespirit.com/the-spiritual-meaning-of-apocalypse/

Showalter, Elaine. Hystories: Hysterical Epidemics and Modern Media. New York: Columbia University Press. 1998.

The 2004 Madrid Train Bombings: Terror, Lies, and Political Fallout. RailTarget. January 27, 2025. https://www.railtarget.eu/passenger/madrid-train-bombings-2004-terrorism-tragedy-10037.html

The Yorkshire Ripper. The Coverup of the Century. June 23, 2025. https://www.yorkshireripper.com/the-story/

What is jihadism? BBC News. December 11, 2014. https://www.bbc.com/news/world-middle-east-30411519

What is the Abrahamic Covenant? Got Questions. June 23, 2025. https://www.gotquestions.org/Abrahamic-covenant.html

Who was David Koresh: Ex-followers describe life inside apocalyptic religious sect involved in 1993 Waco siege. ABC News. January 2, 2018. https://abcnews.go.com/US/david-koresh-followers-describe-life-inside-apocalyptic-religious/story?id=52033937

Winslow, Ben. Rumors of apocalypse ahead of FLDS leader's detention hearing. Fox 13 news. April 5, 2016. https://www.fox13now.com/2016/04/05/rumors-of-apocalypse-ahead-of-flds-leaders-detention-hearing

16: The Late Great Hal Lindsey

An Analysis of Hal Lindsey's "The Late Great Planet Earth." Rogers Website. March 22, 2025. https://www.rogerswebsite.com/articles/AnAnalysisoftheLateGreatPlanetEarth.pdf

Captain Cassidy. The late great Hal Lindsey and the death of a failed prophet. Roll to Disbelieve. January 6, 2025. https://rolltodisbelieve.com/the-late-great-hal-lindsey-and-the-death-of-a-failed-prophet/

Dawkins, Richard. The God Delusion. Boston: Houghton Mifflin Company. 2006.

Delphic Oracle. The Editors of Encyclopaedia Britannica. March 18, 2025. https://www.britannica.com/topic/Delphic-oracle

Esposito, Joey. Mystic Predicted 'End Times' Will Begin in 2025? Snopes. October 28,

2024. https://www.snopes.com/fact-check/mystic-predicts-end-times/

Greenberg, Mike. Psyche: The Goddess of the Soul. Mythology Source. June 2, 2020. https://mythologysource.com/psyche-greek-goddess/

Harris, B. W. Behind the Curtain: The Wizard of Oz's Political Allegory Decoded. Medium. February 19, 2024. https://medium.com/illumination/behind-the-curtain-the-wizard-of-ozs-political-allegory-decoded-2df3c7bd2a74

Herman, Mark C. The Late Great Planet Earth. EBSCO. 2022. https://www.ebsco.com/research-starters/literature-and-writing/late-great-planet-earth

Hutton, Christopher. The Legacy Of Harold Camping, Who Falsely Predicted The World's End, Lives On. Religion Unplugged. May 21, 2021. https://religionunplugged.com/news/2021/5/21/the-legacy-of-harold-camping-who-falsely-predicted-the-worlds-end-lives-on

K, Denisa. Jeane Dixon Predictions That Did and Did Not Come True. Chi-Nese. December 11, 2023. https://chi-nese.com/jeane-dixon-predictions-that-did-and-did-not-come-true/

Lanzendorfer, Joy. 13 Facts About L. Frank Baum's 'Wonderful Wizard of Oz'. Mental Floss. August 30, 2023. https://www.mentalfloss.com/article/66583/13-facts-about-l-frank-baums-wonderful-wizard-oz

Lindsey, Hal. The Late, Great Planet Earth. The Classic Analysis of the Biblical Prophecies Leading Up to the Return of Jesus Christ. Grand Rapids, MI: Zondervan. 1970.

Lundbom, Jack R. Prophets in the Hebrew Bible (or Prophets in the Old Testament.) Oxford. May 9, 2016. https://oxfordre.com/religion/display/10.1093/acrefore/9780199340378.001.0001/acrefore-9780199340378-e-109?rskey=qRMIyZ&result=1

Osborne, Samuel. Baba Vanga: Who is the blind mystic who 'predicted the rise of Isis'? Independent. December 8, 2015. https://www.independent.co.uk/news/world/baba-vanga-who-is-the-blind-mystic-who-predicted-the-rise-of-isis-a6765071.html

Trank, Lisa. Baba Vanga; Bulgarian Mystic's Predictions Parallel Nostradamus.' Gaia. January 23, 2020. https://www.gaia.com/article/baba-vanga-bulgarian-mystics-predictions-parallel-nostradamus

17: Rev. Jim Jones

Barcella, Laura. How Jim Jones Used Drugs to Run Jonestown and Control Members of the Peoples Temple. A&E True Crime. March 18, 2021. https://www.aetv.com/real-crime/jim-jones-drugs-jonestown-control-peoples-temple

Coffey, James R. The Reverend Jim Jones: Profile of a Megalomaniac. History Defined. March 18, 2025. https://www.historydefined.net/jim-jones/

Guinn, Jeff. *The Road to Jonestown: Jim Jones and the Peoples Temple*. New York: Simon and Shuster. 2017.

Jim Jones. World Celebs. March 21, 2025. https://world-celebs.com/celebrity/2156-jim-jones.html

Jonestown. *History*. April 19, 2022. https://www.history.com/topics/crime/jonestown

Jonestown: The Life and Death of People's Temple: Race and the People's Temple.

American Experience. March 17, 2025. https://www.pbs.org/wgbh/americanexperi
ence/features/jonestown-race/

Kennedy, Lesley. Inside Jonestown: How Jim Jones Trapped Followers and Forced 'Suicides.' The over 900 deaths in Guyana under cult leader Jim Jones were more mass
murder than suicide. History.com. August 14, 2018. https://www.history.com/news/
jonestown-jim-jones-mass-murder-suicide

McGinnis, Alan Loy. Bringing Out the Best in People. Minneapolis: Augsburg
Publishing House. 1985.

Melton, J. Gordon. Father Divine. American religious leader. Britannica. March 17,
2025. https://www.britannica.com/topic/monotheism/The-spectrum-of-views-
monotheisms-and-quasi-monotheisms

Mersault, Patrice. An Open Letter from Jim Jones, Leader of the People's Temple, to
MAGA Cultists. How 900 Deaths, Cyanide Kool-Aid, and a Jungle Compound Pale
in Comparison to Your Fearless Leader's Modern Cult Mastery. January 8, 2025.
https://patricemersault.substack.com/p/an-open-letter-from-jim-jones-leader

Scheeres, Julia. *A Thousand Lives: The Untold Story of Hope, Deception and Survival at
Jonestown.* New York: Free Press. 2011.

Speier, Jackie. Undaunted: Surviving Jonestown, Summoning Courage, and Fighting
Back. Boston: Little A. 2018.

Stuckart, Emerson Maureen. Alternative Considerations of Jonestown & Peoples
Temple. *Heidelberg Center For American Studies at the Ruprecht-Karls-Universität-
Heidelberg in Germany.* January 2014. https://jonestown.sdsu.edu/?page_id=61794

The People's Temple: how Jim Jones controlled his followers. Crime Investigation. March
19, 2025. https://www.crimeandinvestigation.co.uk/shows/jonestown-the-women-
behind-the-massacre/the-people-s-temple-how-jim-jones-controlled-his-followers

18 & 19: Y2K and the God Particle

Allen, Frederick E. Apocalypse Then: When Y2K Didn't Lead to The End of Civilization. Forbes. December 20, 2019. https://www.forbes.com/sites/frederickallen/2020/
12/29/apocalypse-then-when-y2k-didnt-lead-to-the-end-of-civilization/

Anslow, Louis. America tried to ban fake photos in 1912.The nation has been wrestling
with manipulated images since long before AI. FreeThink. June 4, 2025. https://
www.freethink.com/the-digital-frontier/fake-photo-ban-1912

Automations in Greek Mythology. April 11, 2025. Greek Legends and Myths. https://
www.greeklegendsandmyths.com/automatons.html#google_vignette

Boston, Rob. False Prophets, Real Profits. AJ Americans United. February 2000. https://
web.archive.org/web/20160927030808/https://www.au.org/church-state/february-
2000-church-state/featured/false-prophets-real-profits

Cartwright, Mark. Top 10 Inventions of the Industrial Revolution. March 20, 2023.
https://www.worldhistory.org/article/2204/top-10-inventions-of-the-industrial-revo
lution/

Clark. 2001: A Space Odessey. London: Hutchingson. 1968.

Curley, Tom. Talos – The Bronze Robot God Of Ancient Greece. History Hogs. December 10, 2023. https://historyhogs.com/talos/

Dow, Cat. The Google Self-Driving Car: All you need to know about Waymo. Car Magazine. October 18, 2022. https://www.carmagazine.co.uk/autonomous/waymo-google-self-driving-car/

Faber, Tom. The Guardian. December 28, 2024. https://www.theguardian.com/technol ogy/2024/dec/28/all-people-could-do-was-hope-the-nerds-would-fix-it-the-global-panic-over-the-millennium-bug-25-years-on?utm_source=join1440&utm_medium= email

Fritscher, Lisa. The Different Types of Doomsday Phobias. VeryWellMind. August 14, 2023. https://www.verywellmind.com/doomsday-phobias-2671856

Fuge, Lauren. Fifty years later, scientists reflect on the influence of 2001: A Space Odyssey

Cosmos. October 17, 2018. https://cosmosmagazine.com/space/fifty-years-later-scien tists-reflect-on-the-influence-of-2001-a-space-odyssey/

Gera, V. Polish radio station abandons use of AI 'presenters' following outcry. Associ-ated Press News. October 28, 2024. https://apnews.com/article/poland-media-radio-ai-bba6beb01d523c6727d650c69da14960

Hammer, Alex. Luigi Mangione's chilling Goodreads page filled with creepy quotes about health. Daily Mail. December 9, 2024. https://www.dailymail.co.uk/news/arti cle-14174963/luigi-mangione-arrest-social-media-unabomber.html

art, Betsy. Christian Y2K alarmists irresponsible. Desert News. February 12, 1999. https://www.deseret.com/1999/2/12/19428637/christian-y2k-alarmists-irresponsible/

How Alan Turing *Cracked the Enigma Code*. IWM. April 11, 2025. https://www.iwm.org. uk/history/how-alan-turing-cracked-the-enigma-code

Jordan. John M. The Czech Play That Gave Us the Word 'Robot.' The MIT Press Reader. April 7, 2025. https://thereader.mitpress.mit.edu/origin-word-robot-rur/

Listopia. Y2K: The Millennium is Here. GoodReads. April 8, 2025. https://www. goodreads.com/list/show/191051.Y2K_The_Millennium_is_Here

Loeb, Zachary. The lessons of Y2K, 20 years later. The Washington Post. December 30, 2019. https://www.washingtonpost.com/outlook/2019/12/30/lessons-yk-years-later/

Loeffler, John. Strangelets won't destroy the Earth, but are still spooky as hell. Inter-esting Science. July 24, 2025.

https://interestingengineering.com/science/strangelets-rhic-and-lhc-controversy-explained?group=test_a

Lowne, Cathy and Bauer, Patricia. I, Robot. Britannica. April 6, 2025. https://www.britan nica.com/topic/I-Robot

Morgan Amanda. BookLash: "Frankenstein." The Wood Word. February 14, 2022. https://www.thewoodword.org/entertainment/2022/02/14/booklash-frankenstein/

Neill, Celeste. The Legacy of Hal 9000: How Science Fiction Depictions of AI Have Changed Over Time. HistoryHit. March 13, 2023. https://www.historyhit.com/culture/the-legacy-of-hal-9000-how-science-fiction-depictions-of-ai-have-changed-over-time/

Nguyen, Tuan C. The History of Computers. ThoughtCo. January 26, 2021. thoughtco.-com/history-of-computers-4082769.

O'Brien, Matt. What is DeepSeek, the Chinese AI company upending the stock market? Associated Press. January 27, 2025. https://apnews.com/article/deepseek-ai-china-f4908eaca221d601e31e7e3368778030

Pappas, Stephanie. Farewell, Tevatron: Giant Atom Smasher Goes Silent After 28 Years. LiveScience. September 30, 2011. https://www.livescience.com/16328-fermilab-tevatron-shut.html

Parvini, S. Robert Downey Jr. says he 'intends to sue' all future executives who use his AI replica. ABC News. October 29, 2024. https://abcnews.go.com/Technology/wire Story/robert-downey-jr-intends-sue-future-executives-ai-115274130

Pitman, Robert. Who Was Robby the Robot? Why He Appeared in 21 Sci Fi Movies & Shows. ScreenRant. February 10, 2024. https://screenrant.com/robby-the-robot-forbidden-planet-explained/

Pope Francis denounces a world 'losing its heart' in the fourth encyclical of his papacy. Associated Press. October 26, 2024. https://apnews.com/article/pope-encyclical-global-conflicts-consumerism-algorithms-love-c9099f3cd0e69b793b4d53eda47c4123

Sanchez, Chelsey. Everything to Know About the SAG Strike That Shut Down Hollywood. Harpers Bizarre. November 9, 2023. https://www.harpersbazaar.com/culture/politics/a44506329/sag-aftra-actors-strike-hollywood-explained/

Shakey the Robot. SRI. April 9, 2025. https://www.sri.com/hoi/shakey-the-robot/

Sheldon, Robert. ENIAC (Electronic Numerical Integrator And Computer). TechTarget. September 2023. https://www.techtarget.com/whatis/definition/ENIAC

The Atom Smashers. PBS. November 25, 2008. https://www.pbs.org/independentlens/documentaries/atomsmashers/

Westworld. IMDb. April 8, 2025. https://www.imdb.com/title/tt0070909/trivia/?ref_=tt_dyk_trv

What to Know If You Feel Anxious About the End of the World. VeryWellMind. August 14, 2023. https://www.verywellmind.com/doomsday-phobias-2671856#:~:text=Doomsday%20phobias%20are%20a%20broad%20category%20of%20pho bias,winter%2C%20while%20other%20people%20are%20afraid%20of%20Armageddon.

Wiggers, Kyle. MIT study finds that AI doesn't, in fact, have values. TechCrunch. April 9, 2025. https://www.yahoo.com/finance/news/mit-study-finds-ai-doesnt-164823370.html

20: The Cyber Deep State

Adams, Brooke. Unabomber: From his tiny cabin to the lack of electricity and water, Kaczynski's simple lifestyle in Montana coincided well with his anti-technology views. Desert News. April 11, 1996. https://www.deseret.com/1996/4/11/19236101/unabomber-from-his-tiny-cabin-to-the-lack-of-electricty-and-water-kaczynski-s-simple-lifestyle-in-mo/

Alex Jones. Southern Poverty Law Center. May 13, 2025. https://www.splcenter.org/resources/extremist-files/alex-jones/

Bailey, Holly. The Unabomber takes on the Internet. Cliff Notes: The Letters. January 28, 2026. https://www.thetedkarchive.com/library/holly-bailey-ted-kaczynski-the-unabomber-takes-on-the-internet

Collins, Dave; Lozano, Juan A.; and Vertuno, Jim. What we know about the fight between conspiracist Alex Jones and Sandy Hook families over his assets. AP News. June 15, 2024. https://apnews.com/article/alex-jones-infowars-bankruptcy-sandy-hook-0c3576e3c4bd853ac2cc5342118fca8c

Egan, Matt. One of America's biggest companies is imploding. CNN. May 15, 2025. https://www.cnn.com/2025/05/15/business/unitedhealth-stock-ceo-investigation

Furek, Maxim W. Coal Region Hoodoo: Paranormal Tales from Inside the Pit. San Diego: Beyond the Fray. 2023.

Gilbert, David. Meet the Antisemitic QAnon Leader Who Led Followers to Dallas to Meet JFK. Vice. November 5, 2021. https://www.vice.com/en/article/qanon-dallas-jfk-michael-brian-protzman-negative48/

Jeffries, Candice. The Truth about Alex Jones. Nicki Swift. January 31, 2023. www.nickiswift.com/99733/untold-truth-alex-jones/

Ramirez, Nikki McCann. Leader of JFK Jr.-Obsessed QAnon Cult Dies After Dirt Bike Accident. Rolling Stone. July 6, 2023. https://www.rollingstone.com/politics/politics-news/qanon-cult-leader-michael-protzman-dies-dirt-bike-accident-1234784194/

Rawat, Megha. Who Was Ted Kaczynski? Luigi Mangione Liked 'Unabomber"Quotes On Goodreads. December 10, 2024. https://www.timesnownews.com/world/us/us-news/who-was-ted-kaczynski-luigi-mangione-liked-unabomber-quotes-on-goodreads-article-116149815

Rumpf, Sarah. FLASHBACK: On Sept. 12, 2001, Alex Jones Blamed the Terrorist Attacks on Israel, Claimed We Would Get 'Nuked', And It Would Be Their Fault. Mediaite. September 11, 2022. https://www.mediaite.com/online/flashback-on-sept-12-2001-alex-jones-blamed-the-terrorist-attacks-on-israel-claimed-we-would-get-nuked-and-it-would-be-their-fault/

Shugerman, Emily. This one internet subculture explains murder suspect Luigi Mangione's odd politics. San Francisco Standard. December 10, 2024. https://sfstandard.com/2024/12/10/this-one-internet-subculture-explains-murder-suspect-luigi-mangiones-odd-politics/

Tabor, Nick. Luigi Mangione: accused murderer. Encyclopaedia Britannica. May 12, 2025. https://www.britannica.com/biography/Luigi-Mangione

Time, Clandis. Was the Unabomber Right or Wrong? The Ted K Archive. October 23, 20243. https://www.thetedkarchive.com/library/clandestime-was-the-unabomber-right-or-wrong

Timotija, Filip. UnitedHealth CEO stepping down. The Hill. May 13, 2025. https://thehill.com/policy/healthcare/5297383-unitedhealth-ceo-andrew-witty-stepping-down/

21: The Drone Hysteria of 2024

Ali, Ayesha and McMichael, Clara. FAA temporarily bans drones in parts of New jersey, New York adds flight restrictions. ABC News. December 20, 2024. https://abcnews.go.com/US/drone-updates-faa-temporarily-bans-drone-operations-parts/story?id=116936091

Bartholomew, Robert E., and Weatherhead, Paul. *Social Panics and Phantom Attackers: A study of Imaginary Assailants*. Singapore: Palgrave Macmillan. 2024.

Chung, Frank. Rogue nuke': Terrifying theory about mystery drones. Technology. December 16, 2024. https://www.news.com.au/technology/innovation/military/rogue-nuke-terrifying-theory-about-mystery-drones/news-story/4edec0a4a655bb b02f1081fdd4dfb919

Fortinski, Sarah. Nothing indicates 'public safety risk' from drone sightings: Kirby. The Hill. December 17, 2024. https://thehill.com/homenews/administration/5043728-john-kirby-public-safety-threats-drones/

Furek, Maxim W. The Drone Hysteria of 2024. Strange Knocks Magazine. April 2025.

Gallup, George. "Nine out of Ten Heard of Flying Saucers." Public Opinion News Service, Princeton, N.J., August 15, 1947.

Hanson, Tom. Why drone hysteria has taken off. CBS News. December 22, 2024. https://www.cbsnews.com/news/why-drone-hysteria-has-taken-off/

Johnson, Stephen. What People are getting wrong this week: The New Jersey Drone Invasion. Lifehacker. December 19, 2024.https://lifehacker.com/entertainment/people-getting-wrong-this-week-new-jersey-drone-invasion

Jones, Kelly. The Pentagon didn't confirm drones are 'not of earthly origin'. December 20, 2024. https://www.wkyc.com/article/news/verify/government-verify/drone-not-of-earthly-origin-fact-check/536-57959d66-222d-4351-8646-29504c24dcf8

Keane, Isabel. NJ senator says feds are too 'fearful' of public reaction to tell the truth about mysterious drones

New York Post. December 15, 2024. https://nypost.com/2024/12/15/us-news/nj-senator-thinks-feds-are-fearful-to-reveal-truth-about-drones/

Lovering, Cathy. All About Apophenia. Psych Central. December 8, 2021. https://psych central.com/health/apophenia-overview

Sager, Monica. Nancy Mace Says Mystery Drones Could be "Craft from Outer Space." Newsweek. December 17, 2024. https://www.newsweek.com/nancy-mace-aliens-drones-ufo-space-government-2002286

Satan In the Smoke? A Photojournalist's 9/11 Story. PRNewswire. September 12, 2011. https://www.prnewswire.com/news-releases/satan-in-the-smoke-a-photojournal ists-911-story-129670653.html

Schwartz, A. Brad. The Infamous "War of the Worlds" Radio Broadcast Was a Magnificent Fluke. Smithsonian. May 6, 2015. https://www.smithsonianmag.com/history/infamous-war-worlds-radio-broadcast-was-magnificent-fluke-180955180/

Wallace, Amanda. Timeline: When drone reports first appeared in NJ and what's happened since. Northjersey.com. December 13, 2024. https://www.northjersey.com/

story/news/new-jersey/2024/12/13/nj-drones-timeline-from-first-appearance-to-now/76958254007/

Watson, Eleanor. What do we know about mystery drones flying over New Jersey, New York, Pennsylvania and other East Coast states? CBS News. December 17, 2024. https://www.cbsnews.com/news/drones-new-jersey-what-we-know/

Weindling, Jacob. What Happened to the New Jersey Drone Panic? Did Everyone Just Go Inside? Splinter. December 27, 2024. https://www.splinter.com/what-happened-to-the-new-jersey-drone-panic-did-everyone-just-go-inside

Wilson, Chad. Decoding the Drone Phenomenon

Alien Craft or Human Tech? Paranormal Underground. December 2024. Vol. 17 (12.) 22-24.

22: Fear Mongering

Chance, Matthew. As Ukraine batters Russia with daring assaults, firebrand pro-Kremlin pundits rattle nuclear sabers. CNN. June 4, 2025. https://www.cnn.com/2025/06/04/europe/nuclear-threat-ukraine-russia-latam-intl

Furek, Maxim W. H.P. Lovecraft. The Haunter of the Dark. *Fate Magazine*, 740. April 2024.

Goldin, Melissa. FACT FOCUS: A look at false and misleading claims made by Trump during his first week back in office. AP News. January 24, 2025. https://apnews.com/article/donald-trump-fact-focus-first-week-president-claims-4b60d31b3209e98e63ec383d3f4052dc

Gurzo, Maranda. When the Stars Will be Bright: HP Lovecraft Between prophecy and Apocalypse. Axis Mundi. June 18, 2020. https://axismundi.blog/en/2020/06/18/when-the-stars-will-be-right-hp-lovecraft-between-prophecy-and-apocalypse/

Joseph Goebbels: On "The Big Lie." Jewish Virtual Library. June 6, 2025. https://www.jewishvirtuallibrary.org/joseph-goebbels-on-the-quot-big-lie-quot

Mueller, Chris. Debunking false, misleading claims about President-elect Trump. USA TODAY. November 26, 2024. https://www.usatoday.com/story/news/factcheck/2024/11/06/donald-trump-misinformation-fact-check/76089352007/

Putin issues nuclear warning to the West over strikes on Russia from Ukraine. Reuters. September 25, 2024. https://www.cnn.com/2024/09/25/europe/putin-nuclear-warns-west-missile-strikes-ukraine-intl-latam/index.html

Turn! Turn! Turn! The Byrds. The Very Best of. Sonichits. June 6, 2025. https://sonichits.com/video/The_Byrds/Turn%21_Turn%21_Turn%21#google_vignette

23: Primal Beast

Davidson, Richard J., & Begley, Sharon. The Emotional Life of Your Brain: How Its Unique Patterns Affect the Way You Think, Feel, and Live--and How You Can Change Them. New York: Hudsoon Street Press. 2012.

Excessive fear. NANDA diagnoses. June 18, 2025. https://nandadiagnoses.com/excessive-fear/

Hicks, J. A., Cicero, D. C., Trent, J., Burton, C. M., & King, L. A. (2010). Positive affect, intuition, and feelings of meaning. *Journal of Personality and Social Psychology, 98*(6), 967–979. DOI: 10.1037/a0019377

Huntington, Charlie. Maslow's Hierarchy of Needs: Definition, Examples & Explanation. Berkeley Well Being. June 19, 2025. https://www.berkeleywellbeing.com/maslows-hierarchy-of-needs.html

Jampolsky, Gerald. *Love Is Letting Go of Fear.* Berkely: Celestial Arts. 1979.

Maslow, Abraham H. Motivation and Personality. New York: Harper & Row.1954.

Oaklander, Mandy. The Science of Bouncing back. Time. May 21, 2015. https://time.com/3892044/the-science-of-bouncing-back/

Overcoming Fear: Three Remedies for Fear; What Buddha had to Say About Fearlessness in Abhaya Sutta. Buddha Weekly. June 19, 2025. https://buddhaweekly.com/overcoming-fear-three-remedies-fear-buddha-say-fearlessness-abhaya-sutta/

Salvo, Victor. Dorothy Thompson. (1893-1961). The Legacy Project. June 18, 2025. https://legacyprojectchicago.org/person/dorothy-thompson

24: The Glimmer of Promise

Dougherty, Kyle. One thought on "A Look Back at "Beat Zen, Square Zen, and Zen" by Alan Watt." Rethinking Religion. May 15, 2024. https://rethinkingreligion-book.info/a-look-back-at-beat-zen-square-zen-and-zen-by-alan-watts/

Esselmont, Brigit. Do Tarot Cards Tell the Future? Biddy Tarot. 2024. https://biddytarot.com/blog/does-tarot-tell-future/

Rotolo, Chip. 30% of Americans Consult Astrology, Tarot Cards or Fortune Tellers. Pew Research. May 21, 2025. https://www.pewresearch.org/religion/2025/05/21/3-in-10-americans-consult-astrology-tarot-cards-or-fortune-tellers/

Watt, Alan. Beat Zen, Square Zen, and Zen.

Southwick, Steven M., & Charney, Dennis S. Resilience: The Science of Mastering Life's Greatest Challenges. New York: Cambridge University Press, 2012.

The Side Effects of Fear. Thoughts By Charles Stanley. Thoughts About God. September 27, 2023. https://thoughtsaboutgod.com/category/men-devotions

ABOUT THE AUTHOR

Author Maxim Furek investigating Point Pleasant, West Virginia, and the site of The Mothman Prophesy (Patricia A. Furek).

Maxim Furek's rich background includes aspects of psychology, addictions, music journalism, and the paranormal. He has a master's degree in communications from Bloomsburg University and a bachelor's degree in psychology from Aquinas College.

Maxim has interviewed celebrity demonologists Ed and Lorraine Warren and white witch Dr. Frederick Lamonte Santee. He was featured on *Coast to Coast* with George Noory, *Exploring the Bizarre* with the legendary Timothy Green Beckley and Tim R. Swartz, and Art Bell's *Midnight in the Desert* with Heather Wade.

Described as a paranormal futurist, Furek is a much-in-demand speaker at paranormal and Bigfoot conferences and is a frequent guest on late-night podcasts. His personal quote is, "Don't allow others to define who you are."

His website is www.maximfurek.com

ALSO BY THE AUTHOR

The Lost Tribes of Bigfoot

Sheppton: The Myth, Miracle, and Music

Flying Saucer Esoteric: The Altered States of Ufology

Somebody Else's Dream: Dakota, the Buoys & "Timothy"

Coal Region Hoodoo: Paranormal Tales from Inside the Pit

The Jordan Brothers: A Musical Biography of Rock's Fortunate Sons

The Death Proclamation of Generation X:
A Self-Fulfilling Prophesy of Goth, Grunge, and Heroin

AFTERWORD

Hangar 1 Publishing is the leader in Bigfoot, cryptid, and UFO publications, and home to the innovative IBT (Immersive Book Technology) that can be found in this book. Go to hangar1publishing.com to learn more about our authors, who are recognized in the field, and for public speaking information.